Make Time

Practical Time Management that Really Works!

Make TIME

Practical Time Management that Really Works!

KRIS COLE

Bax Associates Pty Ltd, Adelaide, Australia
2001

Prentice
Hall

First published 2001

Pearson Education Australia
Unit 4, Level 2
14 Aquatic Drive
Frenchs Forest NSW 2086

Acquisitions Editor: Mark Stafford
Project Editor: Kathryn Fairfax
Copy Editor: Fiona Egan
Cover and internal design: Robert Klinkhamer
Typeset by Midland Typesetters
Cartoonist: Peter Broelman
Printed in Australia

1 2 3 4 5 05 04 03 02 01

ISBN 1 74009 449 2

National Library of Australia
Cataloguing-in-Publication Data

Cole, Kris.
Make Time: practical time management that really works.

Bibliography.
ISBN 1 74009 449 2.

1. Time management. I. Title.

304.23

An imprint of Pearson Education Australia

Contents

CONTENTS

Preface

This book was born out of my own struggles with time management. One day, I found myself responsible for a team of people. My diary system, which had worked so well when I was responsible only for myself, left me floundering. I was surrounded by chaos. I worked hard, really hard, but fell further and further behind. I'd wake up in the middle of the night disheartened and alarmed by all the things I had to remember to do the next day. Something had to change and it was clear it had better be me!

So I read every book and journal article I could find on time management. I attended seminars and training programs. I watched people who seemed to manage their time well and who seemed to be very well organised. I asked a lot of questions and tried out a lot of ideas. Some worked, others I adapted, and others didn't suit me at all.

Then people started asking me for my advice on how to manage their time better. Eventually I began running *Make Time* workshops. Hopefully, this book will reach even more people.

I believe that if we know what we want to achieve and work sensibly towards our goals, we can live a life that fulfils both our career and personal aspirations. I hope *Make Time* will help you do just that.

Make Time will show you practical ways to achieve results with grace, ease and efficiency. You will discover how to accomplish everything that you want and need to do and claim control of your job and your life. You will find out how to Make Time by doing more with less and fine-tuning the way you do things.

If you would like to pass on any practical time management ideas, please contact me at KrisCole@bax.com.au or MakeTime@bax.com.au.

Kris Cole
March 2001

About the author

Industrial psychologist, manufacturing technologist and best selling author, Kris Cole, helps leading organisations reach peak performance and profitability by showing them great ideas, straight-forward strategies and proven techniques to help people work better together and individually.

She draws on 26 years' experience on five continents to help people and teams learn, develop and expand their skills. She shows people how to bring out the best in themselves and each other. The result is improved communication and increased workplace and personal productivity.

Popular topics for Kris's training programs and keynote speeches include:

• Make Time: Practical Time Management that Really Works!
• Crystal Clear Communication
• Managing for Peak Performance: The Double Helix Model for Developing a Peak Performance Workforce
• Achieving Peak Performance: Proven Mindsets for Success

You can find more information at www.bax.com.au.

What others have said:

• Kris is the most informative, motivating, inspirational and interesting presenter I've ever met!
• Kris is awesome!
• The way Kris presents material helps me remember the points better.
• Kris was able to teach me many things I didn't know.
• Kris captured my attention for the full amount of time! I never switched off once!

Other books by Kris Cole

Crystal Clear Communication: Skills for Understanding and being Understood, Prentice Hall, Sydney, 1993 and 2000. Also available in German, Mandarin and Bahasa Indonesian, and an Indian subcontinent edition.

Supervision: The Theory and Practice of First-Line Management, Prentice Hall, Sydney, 1998 and 2000.

Office Administration and supervision: A Text for the New Office Manager, Prentice Hall, Sydney, 1992, with Barbara Hamilton.

How to Succeed at a Job Interview, Gleneagles Publishing, Adelaide, 1991, with Don Cole. First published in 1982 by E.P. Publishing, London.

PART 1

Do you need to Make Time?

'Let him who would enjoy a good future waste none of his present.'

Roger Babson, 1875–1967
US entrepreneur, educator, philanthropist.

Some signs of a life that's 'too busy'

CHAPTER 1

You know you're too busy when ...

The great American 18th century inventor, scientist, philosopher and statesman, Benjamin Franklin, said:

> 'Dost thou love life?
> Then do not squander time,
> for that is the stuff life is made of.'

People who love life want to make every minute count. And in today's fast moving world, it seems we *have* to make every minute count.

Most of us feel under pressure to accomplish all sorts of things: meet deadlines at work, manage hectic households, attend children's important school and sporting events, keep up-to-date in our profession. How can anyone possibly do everything in a day that needs to be done? We'd *like* to, of course, but how can we?

Do you make time count?

How about you: do you make time count?

- Do you achieve everything that you want to and need to achieve in a day?
- Do you sometimes find that you've worked hard on everyone else's priorities and not your own?
- Are you sometimes more concerned with 'looking' or 'keeping' busy than with accomplishing real results?
- After a day of rushing around, do you sometimes realise you really didn't accomplish very much at all?
- Are you ever frustrated that you're expected to 'do more with less', 'get results', and still find time to make improvements to your organisation and spend time with your loved ones?

> 'Counting time is not so important as making time count.'
>
> *James Walker*
> *President of Harvard University,*
> *1853–1860*

Many people would like to contribute more to their communities, spend more time nurturing their families, and take time out for themselves. Yet they find that to be successful in their working lives, they need to sacrifice some of their private lives. Modern living takes its toll. Is this the way it has to be?

Is it possible to find enough time to do all the things we want and need to do? Can we learn to do more with less, achieve more in less time, and lead a rich and fulfilling life?

You know you're too busy when . . .

If you answer 'Yes' to three or more of the following questions, you probably need to find out how to Make Time.

- Do you often wake up tired and weary?
- Do you wake up in the middle of the night thinking about all the things you need to do the next day, or all the things you *didn't* do the day before?
- Do you 'spin your wheels': work hard but never seem to get anywhere?
- Do you sometimes forget to do things you've agreed to do?
- Do you ever let things 'slide' and then 'pay the price'?
- Do you find yourself doing things for everyone else except yourself?
- Do you have a cup of coffee to 'calm down'?
- Do you 'pounce' on items as soon as they land in your in-tray or electronic mail box?
- Do you often feel that you don't even have time to think; that you're so busy 'keeping up' it's hard to stay on top of things?
- Does there seem to be a million things competing for your attention, each demanding to be done *now*?
- Do you try to do everything yourself because it's easier than asking someone else to do them?

It's your choice

How do you decide what you will do? Is it the 'squeaky wheel that gets the grease'? Do you attend to whatever is at the top of your 'in-tray'? Do you allow the latest interruption, telephone call or e-mail to dictate what you will do next?

Whether you know it or not, you regularly make choices about what you will do now, what you will do later, what you will delegate, and even what you will ignore entirely. You constantly choose between all the competing demands on your time. This means you are responsible for how you spend your time, how much you achieve, how stressed and fatigued you feel and, ultimately, the quality and satisfaction of your life.

What will *Make Time* do for you?

In *Make Time* you will find out how to make these choices consciously, based on a clear understanding of your job and life goals and responsibilities.

You will find out how to take control of your job and your life by applying a range of practical techniques to increase your overall efficiency and accomplish more.

Make Time will help you do more with less, get results, and finetune the way you do things. You will discover how to achieve at work and still find time to lead a fulfilling private life.

You will find out two important things:

1. How to avoid squandering your time on trivia and focus your efforts and energy on high priority, big pay-off tasks. This will make you more effective and happier because you will be achieving your goals.
2. How to become more *efficient* so that you can get more done in less time and make time for doing other things you choose to do.

Make Time will help you achieve more, in less time, with less stress and less hassle. Applying its principles will put you in the 'driver's seat'.

'Tomorrow is the most important thing in life. It comes to us at midnight very clean. It's perfect when it arrives and puts itself in our hands. It hopes we've learned something from yesterday.'

John Wayne, 1907–1979
Actor

CHAPTER 2

Your personal vision for a balanced life

The first step towards making your time really count

TRIP!

'A man may be very industrious, and yet not spend his time well. There is no more fatal blunderer than he who consumes the greater part of life getting his living.'

Henry David Thoreau, 1817–1862
US naturalist and author

In his book *Don't Sweat the Small Stuff*, psychologist Richard Carlson pointed out:

'When you die, your in-basket will not be empty.'

Are you one of the thousands of people who feel obliged to work long hours, virtually cancelling out other parts of your life? Or perhaps you just 'put in the hours', waiting for 'going home time', when life *really* begins?

Both of these approaches squander your time and shrivel your satisfaction with life.

To get the most from life, we need to know two things:

• what is important to us
• what we want to achieve.

This helps us create our own personal vision. It propels, supports and inspires us to make our best efforts to do things that will enrich and improve our lives.

What is important to you? Take a step back from the everyday hustle and bustle of your life and think about what really matters most to you.

Values

Values are deep-seated beliefs about what is right and wrong, good and bad, worthwhile and trivial. Many of our values were formed during our childhood, based on our experiences and the messages our parents and other significant people in our lives gave us.

A POINT IN TIME . . .

Jan was brought up in Sydney and in her family, time was important. For example, they considered it insulting and disrespectful to be late. Today, Jan always plans out carefully when she will leave home in order to arrive on time at the various functions and meetings that she attends. Because she sees time as valuable, Jan also tries to make every minute count by always having something to do. She always brings a book to read in case she is kept waiting and plans her days so she can fit in as much as possible.

Her husband Leo thinks differently about time. Raised in Indonesia, he is more used to *jam karet*, or 'rubber time'. 'What's the big deal, ten minutes here or there?' he says. Timeliness is not an important issue to him, except that he was brought up to believe that, for social occasions or for business events with people of similar or lesser status, being 'on time' is a social gaffe! To Leo, enjoying a beautiful sunset is more important than keeping busy.

It isn't surprising that Jan and Leo often disagree over time and how to use it. It means different things to them. They value it differently and use it differently.

The values we hold and the meanings we attach to things help define us as people. They are part of who we are. They're neither right nor wrong; they just *are*.

Values tend to be so much a part of us that we're hardly aware of them. Buried in our subconscious, they silently guide everything we say and do, including how we manage our time.

What do you value?

A number of values are listed in the box on the next page. Please take a moment to circle those that are most important to you. (Add in any that you want to at the bottom.)

SOME VALUES

Looking good	Having lots of material	Being polite
Giving and receiving	'things'	Acknowledgement
affection	Loyalty	Having fun
Being responsible for	Learning	Justice
others	Conservation	Honesty
Helping others	Peaceful relationships	Independence
Physical fitness	with others	Being current and
Achievement	Feeling important	'with it'
Being in control	Following a religion	Being on time
Working hard	Taking risks	Cooperation
Following tradition	Being relaxed and	Commitment
Saying what we think	informal	Participating
Feeling fulfilled	Standing up for what	Humour
Showing compassion	we believe in	Competition
Confidence	Being logical	Generosity
Being enterprising	Dignity	Initiative
Health	Excellence	Friendship
Truth	Integrity	Tenacity
Trust	Purity	Efficiency
Quality	Beauty	Innocence
Wealth	Perfection	Creativity
Consideration	Optimism	Team Spirit
Intelligence	Reliability	Wisdom
Tolerance	Spontaneity	Culture
Growth	Having authority	Mystery
Being part of a group	Education	Discipline
Being respected	Seeing and being seen	Professionalism
Love	Passion	Nourishment
Clarity	Balance	Self-expression
Humility	Determination	Satisfaction
Understanding	Authenticity	Abundance
Order	Freedom	Responsibility
Courage	Success	Harmony
Security	Duty	Contribution
Adventure	Winning	Desire

Progress	Warmth	Talent
Imagination	Knowledge	Luck
Strength	Awareness	Power
Communication	Honour	Dreams
Acceptance	Vision	Intention
Fulfilment	Adaptability	Motivation
Service	Empathy	Celebration
Opportunity	Compassion	
Peace	Flexibility	
Exploration	Enterprise	

Other things I value:

Source: Cole, Kris, *Supervision: The Theory and Practice of First Line Management*, Prentice Hall, 2nd ed, 2000

From those you've circled as important to you, select your ten most important values. Once you've done that, whittle your choice down to your five most important core values.

You might want to stop a minute and think about how these important values affect the choices you make. How do they affect the way you choose to spend your time?

Knowing what you value most is the first component of creating your personal vision by which to manage your time. Knowing precisely what you want to achieve is the second.

The many 'you's'

Most of us have several roles in our lives that give it meaning and purpose: parent, partner, volunteer, and so on. What sort of person do you want to be in each of these roles? How do you want to be thought of as a friend, a neighbour, an employee, a boss?

Invest some time in your future. Write down some words that you would like to be used to describe you in each of your important life roles. Then write down one goal you would like to achieve in each role over the next six to 12 months. (If a role listed below doesn't apply to you, skip it and move on. If any of your roles are not included below, use the boxes at the bottom of page 14 to add in your own.)

Words that describe me as a . . .

Parent	Boss
....	....
....	....
....	....
....	....
Goal	**Goal**
....	....
....	....

Partner	Sister/Brother
....	....
....	....
....	....
....	....
Goal	**Goal**
....	....
....	....

Friend

Volunteer

....
....
....
....

Goal

Goal

....
....

'We lift ourselves by
our thought; we climb upon
our vision of ourselves. If you want
to enlarge your life, you must first enlarge
your thought of it and of yourself. Hold the
ideal of yourself as you long to be always,
everywhere—your ideal of what you long to
attain—the ideal of health, efficiency,
success.'

Orison Swett Marden, 1850–1924
US editor and author

Employee   Another important role

....

....

....

....

Goal   Goal

....

....

Another important role   Another important role

....

....

....

....

Goal   Goal

....

....

'First say to
yourself what you
would be. And then do
what you have to do.'

Epictetus, Circa 55–135 AD
Rome-based Greek philosopher

This is the second component for creating your personal vision for a balanced life. Here's the final part.

The facets of your life

Just as carefully cut facets give a precious gem beauty, sparkle and appeal, a life with many facets can glow with interest, vitality and passion.

As we know,

> *All work and no play makes Jack a dull boy.*

A balanced life is multi-faceted. What are your most important life facets? What do you want to achieve in each of them?

Polishing your facets

Take a moment to select the most important facets of your life and jot down one or two things you would like to achieve in each of them over the next six to 12 months.

My family

....
....
....
....

My physical and mental health and well-being

....
....
....
....

My career

....
....
....
....

My social life

....

....

....

My spiritual life

....

....

....

My community

....

....

....

Another important facet of my life

....

....

....

Another important facet of my life

....

....

....

Your personal vision for a balanced life

'If you don't have a vision for the future, then your future is threatened to be a repeat of the past.'

A.R. Bernard, Clergyman

Knowing what you value as important and what you want to achieve gives you a personal vision for a balanced life. You have begun to create your future. You have also provided yourself with a solid basis by which to make better use of your time.

Set yourself great goals

Now set yourself some clear, challenging and worthwhile goals. These will serve as your inspiration, your guideposts, and your reference points. Think very carefully about the goals you set for yourself because, as we see in Part 4, you will get what you focus on.

HOW TO SET A GREAT GOAL

- Go for short, clear and positive goals.
- Set clear goals that you will be able to keep constantly in the back of your mind.
- Make sure achieving them is within your control.
- State them in specific terms.
- Make them achievable.
- Establish target dates.
- For big or long-term goals, set targets or milestones along the way. Break them up into shorter and easily trackable action goals that are measurable and relatively easy to reach.
- Make sure your goals are supported by your key values.

Your goals are your glimpse of the future. They identify where you want to be and give meaning and motive to your actions. They help you focus your efforts and manage your time purposefully.

SET PERFORMANCE, NOT OUTCOME, GOALS

Avoid goals based on outcomes that you can't control. These expose you to failure. To save yourself possible disappointment, double check that you have set goals over which you have as much control as possible.

17

Outcome Goal	Performance Goal
Win the race	Beat my personal best
Be the highest selling sales rep in the company	Cold call on at least four potential new clients a week
Be respected in my community	Become involved in a local project

Performance goals relate directly on your own efforts. They don't depend on the business environment, other people, the weather, or luck. This helps you control your achievements and draw satisfaction from them.

Your values and goals are your 'Why?' When you find your why, you'll fly!

'You are what your deep driving desire is.
As your desire is, so is your will.
As your will is, so is your deed.
As your deed is, so is your destiny.'

Brihadaranyaka Upanishad
Hindu philosophical treatise

It's only when you are clear about what you want to do with your life that you can build a *Make Time* routine.

How many goals?

To achieve our potential, we need to strike a balance between having too many goals and not enough goals. Over-committing ourselves is stressful and frustrating, while under-committing ourselves restrains us from reaching our destiny and fulfilling our dreams. Around seven goals works well for most people.

Write them down

When you go grocery shopping, do you make a list of what to buy? How about when you have a day off or plan to spend a day gardening and doing household chores? Do you make a list of what you want to accomplish? When you go on holiday, do you write down what to bring and what you want to see and do?

Most of us realise how sensible it is to write things down. It clarifies our thinking and helps us plan. It stops us from wasting time and going off at a tangent, and helps us make sure we haven't forgotten anything.

Research consistently shows that people who write down their goals are far more likely to achieve them than people who just think about what they'd like to achieve. Invest some time to write down what you want from the most important thing of all—your own life!

> 'Make no little plans; they have no magic to stir the blood . . . Make big plans; aim high in hope and work.'
>
> *Daniel Burnham, 1846–1912*
> *US Architect and city planner*

Make them real

Now that you have written down your goals, there are two more things to do. Visualise and emotionalise: *see* and *feel* yourself achieving your goals. Run a 'mental movie' of yourself achieving each of them.

Try to see it looking through your own eyes: Who is there? Where are you? What are you wearing, saying, hearing and doing? How do you feel? If you have trouble seeing this through your own eyes, first see yourself as if from the audience. Run through your 'performance'. Then step into your own shoes and do it from inside yourself. (You can find out more about this process and why it works in Chapter 19.)

SEE WHAT YOU WANT TO HAPPEN

When he was a boy, **Tiger Woods** was asked what he thought about when he was about to hit the golf ball. He replied: 'I think about where I want the ball to go.'

'Once you make a decision, the universe conspires to make it happen.'

Ralph Waldo Emerson, 1803–1882
US writer and philosopher

Keeping your goals short and clear, and visualising and emotionalising them, embeds them in your subconscious. When this happens, you will 'automatically' start moving in the right direction to achieve your vision. Help, ideas and resources will 'suddenly pop up' to help you. You will 'find' ways to turn obstacles into stepping-stones.

'Even though circumstances may cause interruptions and delays, never lose sight of your goal. Instead, prepare yourself in every way you can by increasing your knowledge and adding to your experience, so that you can make the most of opportunity when it occurs.'

Mario Andretti, retired Italian racing driver

Reality check

Can you commit to your vision? Is it realistic? To make sure, check each of your goals. Ask yourself:

- How skilled am I in this area and what skills do I need to develop or strengthen?
- Am I willing to invest my time and energy to achieve this?
- Am I willing to make any sacrifices I need to in order to achieve this? What might they be? Am I *still* willing to make them?
- Is this goal challenging enough?
- What has prevented me from achieving it in the past? Is this still a problem? If so, how will I overcome it?
- Am I clear about what I want? How will I know when I have achieved it?
- Does it 'ring true'? Can I picture myself achieving it?

A goal without an action plan is just a wish

As the cowboy philosopher Will Rogers said:

'Even if you're on the right track,
you'll get run over if you just stand there.'

Do you have any big ambitions or goals that will take some time to achieve? Break them down into smaller action goals.

JOHN NABER'S GOAL

In 1972, John Naber set himself a goal: to win an Olympic gold medal in backstroke in 1976. That was a big goal! And it was only partially within his control. He decided to focus on how to improve his swimming to achieve it.

He resolved to improve his lap speed over 200 metres by four seconds. In swimming, four seconds is a long time and this was still too big a goal. He broke it down again and again until he settled on a goal that he believed was achievable: *Improve my lap speed by 1/1200th of a second each time I dive into the pool.* Over four years, this small improvement would reduce John's lap time by the four seconds he calculated he needed to win gold. (How long is 1/1200th of a second? An eye blink takes 1/500th of a second!)

He then acted on his goal by training morning and night, for two or more hours a session, for ten months a year, over the next four years. Did it work? In 1976, John Naber won four Olympic medals: two gold for the 100 and 200 metres backstroke and a gold and a silver for two other swimming events.

If you still don't know clearly what you need to do to achieve each of your goals, sit down and think each one through. Break them down if necessary and decide what actions you need to take to put yourself on the right track for achieving them. Write these actions down and set a timetable for beginning and completing each one. Put it where you'll see it daily.

Do you want to be elected Club President? Set yourself a goal to attend monthly club meetings and volunteer to help on one committee before the next three months are up. Do you want to have a great relationship with your children? Set a goal to devote one hour on weekdays and three hours at weekends solely to them.

Just do it!

It's no good wishing you'd done something yesterday or hoping you'll find the time or motivation to do it tomorrow. Our power is in the now, in the doing. We have no power over the past. The only power we have over the future is in what we do today.

The first two letters of goal are GO!

Give your goals staying power

You need to be able to carry your goals around with you in your head so they can act as a reference point and guide your decisions. Until you've committed them to memory, write each one down on an index card and review them every morning when you wake up and every evening when you go to bed. This is when your subconscious is most relaxed and receptive.

Another good idea is to read your goals into a tape recorder and play the tape every day—for example, when you're in the car going to and from work—until you've memorised them. You could also turn the most important elements into a screen saver for your PC and rotate them every week.

The idea is to make your personal vision a part of you. You want to imprint it on your brain and embed it in your subconscious. Once your subconscious has assimilated it, it will work to help you achieve it without you even realising it.

Use your values and your goals to create your own future. And remember these eight powerful words: *If it's to be, it's up to me.*

Congratulations!

You now have a personal vision for a balanced life. The next time you're feeling overwhelmed because there is so much to do or there are so many conflicting demands on your time, ask yourself this question:

*'Of all the things I could do, which will help me make
the most progress towards realising my personal
vision and goals?'*

That's where to focus your efforts and channel your time.

'What an immense
power over life is the power
of possessing distinct aims. The
voice, the dress, the look, the very
motions of a person, define and alter
when he or she begins to live for a
reason.'

Elizabeth Stuart Phelps, 1844–1911
US author

CHAPTER 3

Measure your time

How are you currently using your time?

25

Trying to improve the way we manage our time without knowing how we currently spend it is like stabbing at a piñata blindfolded. A very hit and miss affair!

If you're too busy to take stabs in the dark and hope for the best, you'll need to know how you spend your time now. Memory is a poor guide when it comes to assessing how we spend our time. It's easy to forget the time we spend talking to colleagues, making coffee, eating lunch, twiddling our thumbs waiting for something to happen, and so on.

Although former Israeli Prime Minister Golda Meir said

'I must govern the clock—not be governed by it',

you will benefit from becoming a clock watcher for a day or two and completing the Time Logs at the end of this chapter.

All right, you aren't overjoyed at the prospect of completing a Time Log. However, if you make the effort, you'll probably agree that it isn't as big a hardship as you expected. You'll probably also agree that keeping the Time Log pays real dividends in helping you understand how you use your time and where you can easily make improvements.

Completing the Time Log will give you a baseline to figure out what you're doing wrong, what you're doing right, and where your main problems are. Once you know this, you can decide what you need to do to improve. The Time Log will help you find out and analyse how you use your time and how to use it more effectively.

Time Logs

Completing the Time Log

First, photocopy several sheets of the Time Log at the end of this chapter.

Next, decide on the main categories you will use to identify how you use your time. Some possible categories are shown on the next page. If a category is a large one for you, subdivide it; for example, you could subdivide meetings into one-to-one meetings, meetings with your manager, meetings with team members, and so on. Write your choice of categories across the top of the Time Logs. The tenth column is labelled 'other'; use this as a miscellaneous 'catch-all'.

Examples of categories

WORK

a) meetings (one-to-one, with manager, with team members, etc)
b) opening and dealing with mail
c) writing (letters, reports, memos)
d) completing routine paperwork and documents
e) talking on the telephone
f) dealing with e-mails
g) dealing with in-tray
h) handling interruptions
i) dealing with crises
j) thinking/planning
k) travel
l) dealing with customers
m) routine administration
n) reading
o) lunch and other breaks (include 'socialising')
p) downtime (waiting for something)
q) any other important facet of your work.

OUTSIDE WORK

a) meals (with family, friends, work associates)
b) travel
c) grooming
d) socialising (with friends, with family)
e) spending time with family
f) time with children (helping children with studies, playing)
g) volunteer work
h) watching tv
i) sports (attending, participating)

j)   attending the cinema, theatre, concerts
k)   gardening, housework
l)   talking on the telephone
m) reading (for pleasure, professional/trade matters)
n)   working at a hobby
o)   exercising.

Now, complete the Time Log on at least one typical working day (two would be even better). Keep it for your waking hours, both at work and outside work.

Don't change your usual routine, just note down the things you do and when you do them. Tick the box and write explanatory notes in the time column. Try to complete the Time Log as the day progresses. Every time you change activities, pause and note down the time and what activity you are moving on to. When you deal with an interruption, write it down, showing what it is (telephone, incoming e-mail, office visitor, etc) and how long you spend on it.

If you forget to complete the Time Log for a while, don't worry: pause, recall what you've been doing, and note it down. Approximate the length of time you spent on each activity if you can't remember exactly.

In the final column, note your energy level: high, medium or low.

Energy levels

We all have periods of *high energy*, when we're working fast and well. We easily accomplish a lot during these periods and often lose track of time. Nothing is too much trouble or too difficult.

We also have periods of *low energy*, when we aren't as effective as at other times. This may be due to the amount of sugar in our blood, the length of time since we've had a break, the number of interruptions and routine distractions, our stress and physical comfort levels, or how much we're enjoying what we're doing.

Other times are 'in between'.

Example

At 9 am a customer might ring to follow up on an order, so you would write under the 'telephone' column:

TIME	ACTIVITY	ENERGY LEVEL
9.00	Deal with customer query on order.	H

If your energy level were high, you would write an H in the final column.

The call might end at 9.08 am and you go back to going through your in-tray. You might write under the 'other' column:

TIME	ACTIVITY	ENERGY LEVEL
9.08	Deal with in-tray.	H

At 9.13 am, a colleague might come in to discuss a problem on the production line. You might write in the problem-solving column:

TIME	ACTIVITY	ENERGY LEVEL
9.13	Production line problem, discussion with Lee.	M

When you note your activities, think about how you feel: alert, flat, tired, energetic, etc. Use 'High', 'Medium' and 'Low' to describe your energy level in the last column, 'energy level'.

Filling in the Time Log for one or two days will give you a goldmine of information, and it really won't take up much of your time.

In Chapter 6 you will use your completed Time Logs to analyse extensively how you are currently using your time and to find out how you can use it more effectively.

First, we'll overview the Make Time Model.

If you cannot manage your time, what can you manage?

TIME LOG

Activities

WHAT I WAS DOING AT:	①	②	③	④	⑤
__.30					
__.00					
__.30					
__.00					
__.30					
__.00					
__.30					
__.00					
__.30					
__.00					
__.30					
__.00					

⑥ ⑦ ⑧ ⑨ ⑩

OTHER

ENERGY
LEVEL

TIME LOG

Activities

WHAT I WAS DOING AT:	①	②	③	④	⑤
__.30					
__.00					
__.30					
__.00					
__.30					
__.00					
__.30					
__.00					
__.30					
__.00					
__.30					
__.00					

DATE:

⑥   ⑦   ⑧   ⑨   ⑩

OTHER   ENERGY LEVEL

The Make Time Model

CHAPTER 4

The ultimate key to making time

This model has been helping people make time since at least the 1970s. It has survived so long because it works! Most recently popularised by author Stephen Covey, it is a two-dimensional model of how we use our time.

Understanding this model will help you disprove Gresham's Law of Time Management:

The urgent drives out the important.

It will get you off the treadmill of trying to keep up and onto the sanity saver of attending to what is the most important.

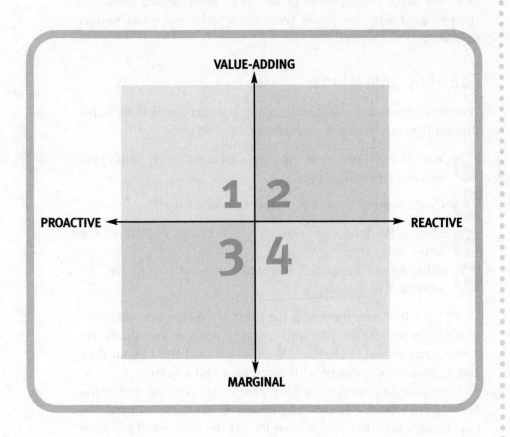

Does an activity add value or is it marginal?

When deciding what to do and setting our priorities, this is the first question we should ask ourselves.

Value-adding activities are those that help you progress towards achieving the goals you established in your personal vision (see Chapter 2). They contribute towards your own and your organisation's success, bring profits, and enrich your life. These are often the tasks we postpone in favour of more urgent ones and then wonder why we never seem to achieve our goals or feel fulfilled by what we do.

Four key questions

Whenever you become aware of something that needs to be done, think it through first. Ask yourself these questions:

1 Will it add any value to my success or my employer's success? (If yes, do it.)

2 Could someone else do it? (If yes, delegate it.)

3 Must it be done right now or can it be done later? (If the latter, delay it.)

4 What would happen if it weren't done at all? (If the sky won't fall in, dump it.)

After a while, you'll develop the habit of quickly assessing how much value something adds and knowing whether you should do it now, later, or not at all. You'll begin to gain control of your time and do what matters most with grace, ease and efficiency.

Value-adding activities are calculated on the vertical axis of the Make Time Model. Use this axis to assess activities on a scale of how much value they add to your life. At the top end of the scale are those activities that most directly contribute to achieving your goals. At the bottom end of the scale are those activities that make little or no contribution to your goals. These are **Marginal** activities.

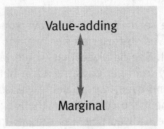

Value-adding

Marginal

Any activity that helps you make progress towards your goals adds value. The closer it moves you to your goals, the more Value-adding it is.

The first and most important thing to know about how to make time is the difference between things you do that add value and things you do merely through habit or because they are urgent.

Focus your efforts on activities that add value.

PULLED IN ALL DIRECTIONS

Martha used to rush around like the proverbial chook with her head cut off. As an internal auditor for a $12 million business and with exceptionally good computer skills and business acumen, she was constantly asked to advise people from all parts of the business on a range of matters. As a mother of three school-age children, she was on call most weekends and some evenings to ferry them to various school and social activities. She tried to cook family meals at least three times a week but often found this impossible. She wanted to exercise more, but could never find the time, and she'd recently given up volunteer work at the local hospital, which she had always enjoyed.

Martha recently attended a *Make Time* workshop where she had an opportunity to really think about how she was managing her time. She was surprised to find out that although she was constantly 'on the move', she actually achieved little of importance.

At work, she seemed to work to everyone's priorities except her own. She resolved to focus on her own job responsibilities and get them done first. She believed that would take some of the frantic busy-ness away from her days, result in better overall job performance, and even free up some valuable time to do more work that would benefit the company in the longer term.

At home, she realised she was caught up in a vicious cycle of day-to-day matters, barely keeping her head above water. She was so busy doing 'chores' and 'errands' that she was letting the things that matter most slip by undone. From now on, she would *make time* to enjoy being with her family. She would *make time* to exercise. And she would *make time* for the volunteer work she used to enjoy so much.

From now on, Martha would be in charge of time, not at its mercy!

Identifying Value-adding activities is important. If we know that something adds value to our lives or work, we will want to do it. If something doesn't add value, why bother doing it unless there's a good reason? (We'll come to what these reasons might be in Chapter 6.)

Make sure you work on at least one Value-adding activity in each of your life roles and facets every day. Since Value-adding tasks are often 'big jobs', you may need to break them down into segments of ten to 20 minutes. Give yourself deadlines for each segment.

Why am I doing it?

Proactive ⟵————————⟶ Reactive

Are you doing something **Proactively**, because you have set out to do it intentionally, or **Reactively**, in response to something else? This is shown on the horizontal axis of the Make Time Model.

Are you doing it automatically?

Do you ever do things because you have to (or think you have to)? Do you do some things automatically or out of habit, or just because 'they're there' (for instance, simply because it's at the top of your in-tray)? If so, you're doing these tasks Reactively. Every time you do something because 'it's there' or through habit, ask yourself:

• What value is this adding?
• How is this moving me closer to my goals?

Are you doing it because it seems urgent?

Some tasks that we do Reactively have some pressure or urgency about them. They must be done *NOW* (or we think they must). For tasks like this, as yourself:

• What would happen if I didn't do this?
• Should someone else do it rather than me?

The curse of reacting

There are three main problems with spending too much time in the Reactive mode. First, we aren't in charge of our own time—something else is! It is usually someone or something else, not us and our goals, that dictates urgency. As a result, attending to urgent tasks seldom moves us any closer to achieving our goals. (How often have you interrupted a discussion or what you were doing to answer the phone, only to find it's a wrong number or a call you didn't really want?) Urgent tasks keep us working hard, but get us nowhere.

> *Don't allow seemingly urgent tasks to keep you busy
> while preventing you from accomplishing something
> more important—something that adds value by
> contributing to your goals.*

So-called urgent tasks not only eat up your time, they add to your stress levels. If you're controlled by urgent tasks, you will probably feel helpless, powerless and not in control. This is stressful.

Finally, attending to urgent matters at the expense of Value-adding activities can force us into a vicious circle. Value-adding activities slide until they become urgent and a 'crisis' develops. That's why 'Reactive mode' is often called 'crisis management'. Many 'crisis managers' find themselves in the mess they are in because they do not attend to matters in a more timely fashion.

Doing things Proactively

When we are in control and deciding which tasks to do now, which to do later, and which not to do at all, we are being 'Proactive'. *We* are in charge, not the environment. Most people prefer to be in charge of their time this way. They can focus their efforts on Value-adding activities that will help them reach their goals.

This is not to say that crises will never develop. We just want them to be as few and far between as possible!

If we don't do things when it's convenient, especially
Value-adding things, sooner or later we will be
forced to do them.

When was the last time something became urgent because you didn't attend to it when you should have?

TAKE CHARGE OF YOUR TIME . . .
OR ELSE!

One of Blake's favourite conference venues was a large resort and conference centre near Perth. Over many visits, he had come to know and respect Richard, the manager. Blake marvelled at the fact that although the centre was large and his duties were many and varied, Richard never seemed 'fazed' by anything. He'd walk around calmly, overseeing and observing, stopping to chat with guests and staff members alike. Things seemed to happen effortlessly and on time. The staff were clearly devoted to Richard and year after year the same faces welcomed Blake back.

One day, Blake arrived to find that Richard had received a big promotion to an even larger resort and had been replaced by two managers. He also found that the conference room hadn't been set up as he'd requested, morning tea and afternoon tea didn't arrive on time, lunch was late, and dinner took far too long to serve.

The two 'managers' rushed around with a look of panic on their faces, never stopping to ask Blake whether everything was all right. He noted the fact that one of them brought the morning tea himself, hot and flustered, after Blake rang reception (20 minutes after it was due) to ask where it was.

The only staff member Blake recognised on this trip was the evening cleaner. 'What happened?' he asked? 'Everyone's gone, the new employees look miserable, nothing happens smoothly as it used to— the place has fallen apart!'

'Tell me about it', she said. 'The only reason I'm still here is I can't find another job! These two clowns have no idea!'

What was the difference? On the surface, the two new managers actually seemed to work harder than Richard. Sadly, effort and results don't always equate.

Richard did things based on how much value they added. He knew what his priorities were and he targeted his efforts at them. This allowed him to take things in his stride.

The two new managers were crisis managers. They stabbed blindfolded at the piñata, rushing around doing everyone's job but their own and failing to attend to important matters. They exhausted themselves and accomplished nothing. They couldn't 'get their act together' because they failed to manage their time, and therefore their energy and their jobs, properly.

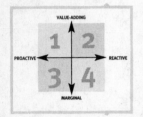

The four quadrants of the Make Time Model

Management guru Peter Drucker (1909–) said:

*'Do not believe that it is very much of an advance
to do the unnecessary three times as fast.'*

How do we know what is *necessary* to do? This is where the Make Time Model and the four key questions posed on page 36 come in.

The Value-adding—Marginal continuum combines with the Proactive—Reactive continuum to form four Quadrants that describe how we use our time. The Quadrants help us understand why we are doing the things we are doing (Proactive or Reactive) and decide whether or not we are doing things that will help us progress towards our goals (Value-adding or Marginal).

Value-adding activities

Quadrant 1

Quadrant 1 activities are **Value-adding** activities that we do **Proactively** because we decide to do them.

Here are some typical Quadrant 1 activities:

AT WORK:
• routine maintenance
• planning
• training staff
• learning new skills
• conducting a safety audit
• prospecting for new customers
• building relationships with staff and customers.

AT HOME:
• building relationships with friends and family
• taking time to relax and unwind

- fixing a loose tread on your stairs
- preparing a healthy meal
- exercising.

> Remember Richard, the manager of the resort in Perth?
> He was a Quadrant 1 manager.

Although these activities add value, they are, unfortunately, very easy to let slide. Here are two reasons we let Quadrant 1 activities slide:

- There is no immediate penalty for not doing them.
- Many people consider Quadrant 1 activities to be difficult. Certainly many of them do require a bit of thought and effort: planning, staff training, and preparing a healthy meal, for instance. Others—for example, taking time to relax and unwind, and exercising—require willpower.

What happens, though, if we let Quadrant 1 activities slide? They eventually turn into a crisis! They move across to Quadrant 2! Here are some examples of situations that might occur if we neglect Quadrant 1 activities:

- We must deal with a piece of equipment that has crashed.
- We eventually pay the price for poor planning.
- We're *forced* to do some staff training.
- A key staff member resigns.
- We fall behind in our professional skills and our value in the job market drops.
- Someone has an accident.
- We lose a good customer to a competitor.
- Our business shrinks or stagnates.
- Our social life fades away.
- We become ill through self-neglect.

Quadrant 2

Quadrant 2 contains **Value-adding** activities that we do **Reactively**. Some typical Quadrant 2 activities are:

AT WORK:
- dealing with an equipment breakdown
- dealing with walk-in customers
- dealing with some telephone calls
- troubleshooting
- doing an urgent job the boss requests
- dealing with someone who has had an accident
- dealing with a special urgent request from a customer.

AT HOME:
- spending a day in bed because we're ill
- spending unplanned time with a family member to repair a ruptured relationship
- dealing with the stairs which have finally become dangerous
- dealing with a special urgent request from a friend.

Some activities, like walk-in customers and important telephone calls, begin as both Value-adding and urgent. Many Value-adding activities, though, *become* urgent through neglect. In fact, most Quadrant 1 activities that we do not attend to in a timely fashion will eventually move into Quadrant 2. How does this happen?

Here are some reasons:

- We lack the self-discipline or self-confidence to attend to Quadrant 1 activities *before* they become a crisis.
- Some people may have a (bad) habit of suddenly asking us to do important rush jobs. (Perhaps they are poor time managers themselves!)
- We may work or live in an unpredictable environment that makes planning difficult.
- We enjoy 'firefighting'!

At what cost?

Let's look at the consequences of working in Quadrants 1 and 2.

44

Quadrant 1 Consequences	Quadrant 2 Consequences
You are in control.	You are not in control, which causes stress.
Things happen in a timely fashion, at your convenience.	Urgent activities may build up and overwhelm you.
Important matters get done.	Important matters get done, but often less well, because of the time pressure involved.
You decide what you will do when, which allows you to make best use of your time.	You may use your time poorly.
You can take a steady, deliberate approach.	You think less clearly.
You can approach things calmly.	You're always rushing around.
Lots of job and life satisfaction.	Less job and life satisfaction.

No-one can avoid Quadrant 2 tasks. As you can see, though, Quadrant 1 is a more 'serene' and empowered place from which to operate. In Part 2, you'll find out how to approach things so that you spend as much time as possible in Quadrant 1.

Marginal activities

Let's turn to the **Marginal** activities in Quadrants 3 and 4. All jobs have them! And sadly, most of us have them in our private lives, too.

What do you do that adds little value to your job or your life? Whenever you're doing one of these activities, you're operating in Quadrant 3 or 4.

PULLING TOGETHER

When Martha decided to take better control of her time so she could achieve more of what she wanted, her first step was to get her job under control. She listed her main areas of responsibility and top priorities, agreed on them with her boss, and used this list to decide what she would do now, what she would do later, what she would delegate to others, and what she would say 'No' to.

Then she began organising her private time. Instead of hopping into the car to ferry children whenever they asked, she helped them organise shared lifts with other nearby families and agreed a schedule with them. As well as freeing up some time, this had the additional benefit of helping her children understand that time was valuable and could be organised.

She also decided to spend three evenings a week cooking a meal with one of her children, which gave them time alone together as well as meeting her goal of cooking a family meal at least three times a week. The children were allowed to select the meals and develop a shopping list for needed ingredients.

She set Saturday afternoons aside for sporting activities and exercise for herself and contacted the hospital association for details on their volunteer program. She set a goal for herself of giving three hours a week of her time to one of these programs.

Quadrant 3

When we're in Quadrant 3, we're working **Proactively** on activities that add *little value*. These are often pleasant activities we enjoy, or activities we escape into to avoid doing other more difficult or less enjoyable activities. Some typical Quadrant 3 activities are:

- trivia
- 'futsing' on the computer
- returning some phone calls
- some 'on-the-job socialising'
- attending some meetings
- 'pouncing' on e-mail and items dropped into your in-tray
- some types of (unnecessary) 'housekeeping' at work
- some telephone calls
- 'administrivia' and unnecessary paperwork
- some administrative tasks (eg filling out expense claims).

Wait a minute! Expense claims are important, aren't they? In one sense, yes they are—you want to be reimbursed! But does filling out an expense claim *really* contribute to any of the goals you are trying to achieve in your job? Unlikely.

This only goes to show that some **Marginal** jobs need to be done! More about this in Chapter 6.

In the meantime, let's look at how we find ourselves wasting time on activities that belong in Quadrant 3.

Here are some possible reasons:

- We accept 'monkeys': we decide to help someone out, leaving our own work undone while we work to other peoples' priorities!
- We do things we enjoy, even though they don't really contribute to our goals (although we might fool ourselves that they do).
- We use some tasks as 'relaxation'.
- We have no-one to delegate these tasks to.
- We fail to delegate the tasks.
- We do **Marginal** tasks because we know we can do them. They are easy to do and give us a (false) sense of satisfaction. Meanwhile, our *real* work is left undone.

Taking an 'on-the-job' break with a Quadrant 3 activity can be a good idea. It can allow us to 'knock off' one or two relatively unimportant but necessary tasks or provide a change of pace. It's when we overuse Quadrant 3 activities, for light relief or as an excuse to avoid other more meaningful activities, that we run into trouble with time.

WHAT HAVE MONKEYS GOT TO DO WITH MAKING TIME?

In 1974, William Oncken, Jr and Donald L Wass presented an analogy for people who fail to assign, delegate and properly supervise their staff's work. First published in the *Harvard Business Review* (November–December 1974) it identified the phenomenon of 'Monkey Management'.

Oncken and Wass called doing the work of others, especially direct reports, 'monkeys'. Every time someone says, '*Hey, what do you think I should do about X?*', and you say, '*Let me think about it*', you've accepted a monkey: someone else's work. Every time someone says, '*Gee I've got this problem and I'm not sure what to do*', and you say, '*Leave it with me*', you've accepted a monkey. Every time someone says '*What do you think we should do about Y?*' and you say '*I'll think about it and get back to you*', you've accepted a monkey. Someone else's responsibility has hopped from their back onto yours.

How many monkeys are hanging onto your back right now?

Quadrant 4

When we're working in Quadrant 4, we're working **Reactively**, because we *have to*, on **Marginal** activities that don't add much value.

Some typical Quadrant 4 activities are:

- dealing with some 'visitors' (in the office or at home)
- some meetings
- some telephone calls
- working to other people's priorities
- doing someone else's work for them (a direct report's, or a colleague's work, or another family member's chores, for example) because they've become urgent

- running 'errands', for example, going to the stationery store for supplies
- dealing with routine 'administrivia' which makes its way to the top of the pile and which you feel obliged to do.

THE SQUEAKY WHEEL
GETS THE GREASE

Bert is a maintenance engineer in an engine factory. His main function is to fix machinery quickly if it breaks down. Since idle machinery costs money, Bert must attend to breakdowns quickly and get the machines working again quickly. He spends most of his working life in Quadrant 4! A lot of customer service workers and carers of young children spend large chunks of time in Quadrant 4, too. The unpredictable nature and pressure to react quickly can make this type of work stressful.

Liz also spends a lot of time in Quadrant 4. Unlike Bert, customer service people and carers of small children, she doesn't have a good reason. She is an administrator who could plan her days if she wanted to. Instead, she's more like a feather being blown around at the whim of the wind. She attends to whatever crops up, whatever grabs her attention or gets into her field of vision. She hops from one job to another, never fully completing anything, always behind, always rushing to meet a deadline. She never feels 'on top' of things, and, consequently, her morale and self-confidence are suffering. Liz's stress is of her own making.

How does it happen that we find ourselves doing Marginal activities under pressure? Here are a few things that can thrust people into Quadrant 4:

- Too many interruptions.
- Lack of self-discipline to do more Value-adding, possibly more 'challenging', activities.

- Letting Value-adding work slide while we attend to more pressing work in Quadrant 4 in the mistaken belief that it is also more important.
- Failing to delegate or having no-one to delegate to, and reasoning that *somebody* needs to do these tasks.
- Others are unclear about our role or priorities and ask us to do Quadrant 4 activities that don't really progress us towards our own goals and should probably be done by someone else.

TWO MONKEYS

Remember the two managers who replaced Richard at the Perth resort? They worked almost exclusively in Quadrants 3 and 4. For example, when morning tea didn't arrive, one of them delivered it himself.

Are you thinking, 'Delivering the morning tea was urgent and needed to be done'? Yes, and who should have delivered it? The managers' job is to manage the restaurant staff. It's the restaurant staff's job to deliver morning tea. Instead of doing someone else's job for them, they should first have the morning tea delivered by the people whose job this is, and then take some action to make sure the system won't break down again.

If you ever feel rushed and out of control, remember the words of the US columnist Sydney J Harris:

'The time to relax is when you don't have time for it.'

Working on Marginal Quadrant 3 and 4 activities has its consequences.

Quadrant 3	*Quadrant 4*
Consequences	*Consequences*
Enjoying what you're doing but achieving little	Harassment and stress
Possibly feeling 'guilty' about leaving more important work undone	Feel victimised
	Dependent on someone else to tell you what to do
	Not in control

Time-wasting

Working hard, achieving little

Jobs that need doing don't get done

Little self or staff development

Difficult and/or Value-adding work is not attended to

'Wheel-spinning'

Poor results

Loss of control

Wouldn't it be nice . . .?

Wouldn't it be nice if we could spend most of our time in Quadrant 1 and a little bit in Quadrant 3 when it suited us? Unfortunately, reality gets in the way! Things that need to be done will always pop up in Quadrants 2 and 4.

It's a question of balance and mix. The mix of time spent in each Quadrant is different for different lives and different jobs.

What is the best mix for your life and your job? To find out, you'll need to analyse your completed Time Logs to see in which Quadrants you're spending most time in the various facets of your life.

PART 2

How to become more effective

'Until one knows how to spend one's time, one cannot hope to manage it.'

Peter Drucker,
Management researcher and author

Know what adds value

CHAPTER 5

How to focus your efforts

I DON'T UNDERSTAND IT. I NEVER SEEM TO GET ANYTHING DONE

'Determine never to be idle. No person will have occasion to complain of the want of time who never loses any. It is wonderful how much may be done if we are always doing.'

Thomas Jefferson, 1743–1826
Third President of the US

Is Thomas Jefferson right? *Should* we always be doing? Or are you thinking: 'Wouldn't it be great if I had the luxury to *not* be always doing?'

How do you spend your time? How *should* you spend it?

Professor Elizabeth Kübler-Ross said:

'It is only when we know and understand that we have a limited time on earth and that we have no way of knowing when our time is up—that we will begin to live each day to the fullest, as if it were the only one we had.'

How can we make better use of our time without the horror of having a death sentence imposed on us? Here's what Lee Iacocca, the retired chair of Chrysler, said:

'If you want to make good use of your time, you've got to know what's most important and then give it all you've got.'

If we want to make the best use of our time, we need to know what adds value.

In order to achieve the results we are paid to achieve at work and the results we want to achieve in our private lives, we need to focus our attention and efforts on important matters. We already know that anything that moves us towards one of our goals, in any facet of our life, is worth doing.

> *Don't wait until your child's wedding day to wish*
> *you'd spent more time with them growing up.*
> *Know what your priorities are.*

Key Result Areas

To really pinpoint activities that will move us towards our goals, we need to identify our Key Result Areas, or KRAs. These are our foremost areas of responsibility and accountability. Most jobs have between five and seven KRAs. We have KRAs in our private lives, too. Each facet of our life that we believe is important will probably have around four KRAs, some more than that, others less.

Three things Key Result Areas are not:

 KRAs are not tasks or activities, nor are they goals. They don't describe what a person does or hopes to achieve. They are *areas* that we must attend to if we are to reach our goals. Let's look at work first and then move onto our private lives.

These are all individual tasks, or activities, *not* KRAs:

- stock taking
- staff training
- completing a health and safety audit
- equipment maintenance
- setting up a display.

They might fall under these KRAs:

Activity	KRA
Stock taking	Stock management
Staff training	Staff leadership
Completing a health and safety audit	Health and safety
Equipment maintenance	Plant/Equipment
Setting up a display	Presentation

Each KRA could have several goals and dozens of tasks and activities that contribute to achieving the goals.

Here are some activities and two KRA headings that might fall under the physical and mental health facet of our private life:

Activity	KRA
Jog each weekday morning Daily 15-minute weight training, upper body	Fitness
Bushwalking, bi-monthly	Fitness and relaxation
Yoga, three times a week 'Veg out' in a bubble bath once a week	Relaxation

2 KRAs do *not* describe what a person is like. They are not qualities or attributes. For example, people whose jobs involve selling, may need to be 'articulate', but they are paid for the sales they generate, not their language skills.

3 KRAs do *not* describe what a person knows. For example 'product knowledge' is not a KRA. It is certainly expected that we have product knowledge in order to do our job. However, we are not paid for our product knowledge but for the results we are able to attain as a result of it. It is expected that a parent is compassionate and can do basic arithmetic, but what counts is whether they cuddle their children when they're sad, and use their knowledge to help their children with their homework.

Here are the KRAs of Mary, a retail store manager:

Customer service		Store presentation
Staff leadership	**Retail Store Manager**	Stock management
Profitability	Administration	Customer relations

Notice the KRAs consist of just one or two words. They describe areas Mary is expected to get results in. They are all equally important. If she fails in one area, her entire job will be adversely affected.

THE QUESTION THAT MAKES TIME

The job of a retail store manager is hectic. Whenever the work piles up and Mary begins to feel overwhelmed by all the things she has to do, she pauses and looks at the above diagram showing her work KRAs. Then she asks: 'What is the best use of my time *right now*?'

She turns her attention to whatever will make the biggest contribution to achieving goals in one of her KRAs.

Mary also has goals for each KRA in her job as a retail store manager. For example, her goals for the KRA of 'Staff leadership' are:

• Speak informally with each staff member at least once a day.
• Set a good example and practise what I 'preach'.
• Carry out formal progress discussions every six months and offer informal feedback at least weekly.

Here are the KRAs in Mary's mental and physical health facet of her life:

Relaxation	Fitness
Mental & Physical HEALTH	
Healthy lifestyle	Healthy food

KRAs KEEP US ON TRACK
AND MOTIVATE US

Whenever Mary feels her life is getting out of balance and becoming too hectic or busy-but-empty, she reviews the KRAs of her life facets in order to focus her attention and keep motivated.

For example, she sees 'Fitness' and instantly is reminded of her weekday jogs, a short burst of daily weight training, and two bushwalks a week. This helps her to get 'back on track'.

Mary knows what she wants to do in each of her KRAs for mental and physical health, as well as for each of the other KRAs relating to the other important facets of her life. For example, her goals for the KRA of 'Healthy food' are:

• Eat three balanced meals a day.
• Eat two pieces of fruit a day.
• Drink two litres of water a day.
• Cook with fresh ingredients at least three times a week.

Pay attention to, and get results in, *each* of your KRAs.
What are the KRAs of your job?

My Key Result Areas

My Job *Title:* _____

Don't worry if you have six or eight KRAs. If your job is full time, you are unlikely to have less than five. If you have more than nine, you could probably combine some KRAs. If this isn't possible, perhaps too much is expected of you. If this is the case, you will find it difficult to meet expectations and you should discuss this with your manager.

In fact, it would be a good idea to discuss your KRAs with your manager if you haven't already done this. It's amazing how often people have different ideas of what is important in a job!

WHAT HAPPENED TO MICHAEL

Michael's first job after completing his business qualification involved writing position specifications, or job descriptions. He diligently interviewed people representing every job in the factory and administration block, job by job. After hours of detailed interviews, he carefully wrote up the job descriptions. To make sure that he had accurately reflected what they had told him, he showed them to the jobholders, who generally seemed satisfied with what he'd written. Then he went to the supervisors of each job to have the job descriptions 'signed off'.

He quickly became used to hearing 'Oh no, that's not the job at all! No! They shouldn't be doing *that*! They should be doing *this*!'

At first, Michael felt that he must have made some terrible mistakes and completely misunderstood the jobholders' descriptions of their jobs. Then he realised that he *had* accurately written down what the jobholders told him their work involved.

He began asking the supervisors whether they had ever sat down and discussed people's main areas of responsibilities with them, and the results they were expected to achieve. Most of the time, the answers were: 'No, of course not—they know what I expect!'

Michael felt disillusioned, but wiser. Everyone, he realised, needs to take responsibility for making sure they clearly understand what the boss expects of them. So he arranged for a series of meetings between groups of employees and their managers to discuss their KRAs and agree goals, or measures of success, within each KRA.

In no time, everyone was working 'off the same page' and things went much more smoothly. Employees no longer toiled away at tasks their supervisors felt were unimportant and unintentionally left Value-adding tasks untouched. They knew what would add value and could focus their energies and efforts accordingly. They could accurately assess how well they were doing their jobs. They felt more satisfied with their work and the positive reactions they were getting from their supervisors.

DO WE NEED TO LOVE THEM ALL?

We all have to do some things in both our private and our working lives that we'd just as soon not do. That's life! For instance, some people hate routine administration, but it still needs to be done. The trick is to find a job that doesn't require too much of it or that allows you to delegate it to someone else. Some people don't like exercise, but do it anyway, knowing that it's important for staying healthy and living longer.

The Key Result Areas in the facets of my life

Referring to your life plan, list your KRAs in your private life. You may want to write your goals, from Chapter 2, underneath each.

Key facet of my life: _____

Key facet of my life: _____

Key facet of my life: _____

Key facet of my life: _____

You decide!

CHAPTER 6

Do it now, do it later, or do it never?

Set your priorities with your Key Result Areas

Here is where you really begin to make progress in making time.

Now that you have identified your Key Result Areas, you can use the Make Time Model to grade the things you do on a scale of importance. You can easily distinguish between what adds value and what doesn't by using the method of analysis that follows.

How are you using your time?

To analyse your Time Log quickly and easily, you will need three different colours of highlighters.

First analysis: Highlight the Value-adding activities on your Time Log

Go back to your Time Log. For each activity you listed, decide whether it did or did not contribute to results in one of your Key Result Areas. (To keep things simple, don't worry about the degree of contribution the activity made. If it contributed, consider it Value-adding. If it didn't contribute or made very little contribution, consider it Marginal.)

Use one colour to highlight the boxes of all the Value-adding activities on your Time Log, whether these were in your home life or working life.

The pattern of highlighted boxes will give you a feel for how much of your time you are spending on Value-adding matters. These are the things that will provide the most pay-off in terms of results. Are you spending enough time doing things that matter? What is the balance between Value-adding and Marginal activities? Is it 'right'? Is it enough to satisfy you and get the results you want?

Perhaps in some areas you are managing to spend a lot of time adding value and in others areas not much at all. For example, many of your meetings may add value, while much of your writing doesn't. Or perhaps your activities add a lot of value at work but little in your private life. Why is this? Do you need to alter this in any way?

No-one can spend 100 per cent of their time on Value-adding activities. We all need breaks if we are to be effective. Sometimes, doing a Marginal activity can be a good break. Balance your day according to your values, needs and moods. Choose how to most effectively spend your time.

TWO MILLION-DOLLAR QUESTIONS

Here are two important questions you need to answer: *Is the proportion of time I am spending on Value-adding tasks enough to:*

1. achieve the results I am paid to achieve in my job?
2. make me feel good about my job and my life in general?

Sit back, relax, and consider these questions for a while.

Second analysis: Circle things you did Proactively

With a second colour highlighter, put a circle in the boxes where you did things Proactively—because *you* set out to do them. Don't circle anything because it had to be done *now* or because events or someone else caused you to do it.

The boxes with circles indicate activities you *chose* to do when it suited you. They show how much time you're spending on your own volition. The more boxes with circles you have, the less stressed, harassed and pressured you are likely to feel, both at home and at work.

Some of the boxes may have been highlighted because they were Value-adding. Highlighted boxes with circles indicate your Quadrant 1 activities. The more of these you have, the better you are managing your time.

Are any highlighted activities not circled? This indicates you did them Reactively. They are Quadrant 2 activities. Could you have done them earlier, when it suited you better? Would you have done a better job?

How much of your time are you spending reacting to outside events and people? The higher the proportion of time you spend on these uncircled activities, the more stressed-out and harassed you are likely to feel. Are you spending too much time Reactively?

Third analysis: Underscore monkeys

Now have a look for monkeys. With the third colour highlighter, underscore boxes representing things you did that were more properly someone else's job, whether at home or at work.

How many monkeys are on your back? If you have discovered a lot of monkeys and you would rather not get a licence to operate a zoo, pay special attention to Chapter 14.

Fourth analysis: Pinpoint the Quadrant

This will really increase your understanding of how you are spending your time. It will also show up some of the time management problems you are struggling with, and help you decide which chapters in Part 3 to focus on first.

Referring to your completed Time Logs, transfer each of the things you did into their Quadrants in the Make Time Model on page 68. Note down:

- all the Quadrant 1 activities you carried out in Quadrant 1. (These are the boxes that are both highlighted in colour 1 and have a circle in colour 2.)
- all the Quadrant 2 activities you did in Quadrant 2. (These are boxes highlighted in colour 1 but have no circle.)
- all the Quadrant 3 activities you did in Quadrant 3. (These are boxes with circles in colour 2 but not highlighted.)
- all the Quadrant 4 activities you did in Quadrant 4. (These are boxes without any highlights or circles.)
- If you underlined an activity on your time log because it was a

monkey, underline it again below. Do your monkeys have any patterns?

This will give you a strong understanding of how you are spending your time and a good idea of how you can begin to make more time.

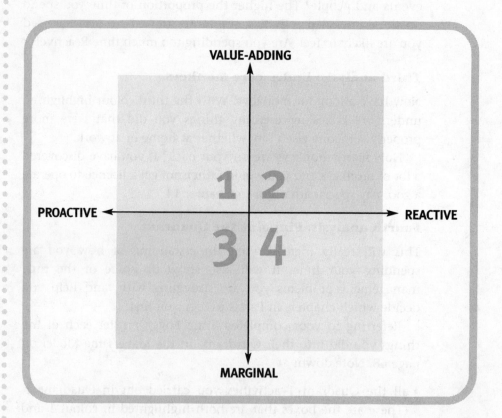

TWO MORE MILLION-DOLLAR QUESTIONS

1. Thinking about what your job and lifestyle require, what is a good mix between the Quadrants for you?
2. How does this compare with how you are currently spending your time?

Fifth analysis: Look for patterns in your energy level

Don't make the mistake of letting the clock rule your life. Many people find their energy levels cycle up and down predictably during the course of the day. Knowing this, they can plan to tackle difficult jobs, or jobs requiring a lot of mental or physical energy, when they are at their best. This increases their efficiency and effectiveness and makes it easier to achieve the results they're looking for.

'Three o'clock is always too early or too late for anything you want to do.'

Jean Paul Sartre, 1905–1980
French philosopher and novelist

Do you notice any patterns forming in your energy levels? For example, does your energy seem to be highest early in the morning? Late in the afternoon? In the early or late evening? These periods of peak energy are your 'prime time'. When does your Time Log suggest you should be tackling your most demanding tasks?

Take charge of your time!

The most common problem with managing time is having too much to do. If we can't do *everything*, what should we do?

By now, the answer should be clear:

> *Do whatever helps you achieve results in any facet of your life or in your job.*

'Things which matter most must never be left at the mercy of things which matter least.'

Johann Goethe, 1749–1832
German poet and dramatist

Rule No 1: Don't feed monkeys!

(1) Try not to do things unless they directly contribute to your Key Result Areas and goals.

(2) At home and at work, channel tasks where they belong.

(3) Don't accept monkeys! If people need help, show them how to do it, don't do it for them!

(4) If your boss, the system, or your life circumstances continually impose work that doesn't directly contribute to your KRAs, discuss this with your manager (if it's a work problem) with a view to achieving one of three things:

(a) altering your KRAs

(b) fixing the system

(c) channelling the work to a more appropriate person.

Or if the problem is in your private life, discuss it with your family or friends to:

(a) distribute tasks more widely

(b) make sure everyone understands who is responsible for doing what

(c) make it clear you won't be responsible for doing other people's tasks.

Rule No 2: Apply the 4 Ds

When work comes in, ask yourself: Should I:

• deal with it now
• delegate it
• delay it
• dump it?

In other words, will it contribute to my own or someone else's overall Key Result Areas? If it contributes to your own KRAs, deal with it! If it contributes to someone else's, delegate it! If it doesn't add much value, should you delay doing it until a more convenient time? Does it need to be done at all? If not, dump it!

Do you think it's dangerous to delay something if it's urgent? Ask yourself: 'What will happen if I don't do it now?' If the result isn't disastrous, you can probably delay it. Maybe you can even dump it! A lot of what we accept as urgent really isn't.

Types of time: Who's *pulling* your *strings*?

Henry Mintzberg of Canada's McGill University studied how people at work spent their time. He found we have three types of time: boss-imposed time, system-imposed time and self-imposed time.

Boss-imposed time

Activities or tasks that our boss requires us to do fall into the category of boss-imposed time. We can't ignore them because if we do, we'll be in strife!

Sixth analysis: Pinpoint your boss-imposed activities

At work, these will be activities you carried out at your manager's request. At home, this will be an 'important other' person that you want to please.

With one of your coloured highlighters, place a symbol such as an asterisk (*) beside each activity you've entered on your Make Time Model (or on your Time Log) that was boss-imposed.

What does this tell you? Does 'the boss' assign Value-adding tasks, or Marginal tasks? If the latter, would it benefit you to discuss this? Perhaps if 'the boss' understood how doing these inconsequential tasks interfered with your ability to attend to more important matters, he/she would assign them to someone more appropriate.

System-imposed time

The 'system' also requires us to do things and if we don't do them there will be penalties! At work, these are often routine administrative tasks such as filling out time sheets, expense sheets, and customer reports. At home, system-imposed tasks include filling out tax and other government forms, paying bills, and putting out the rubbish.

Seventh analysis: Pinpoint your system-imposed activities

With a coloured highlighter, mark each box representing a system-imposed activity on your Make Time Model on page 68 or Time Log with a symbol such as a star.

These must be done, so perhaps you'll need to 'grin and bear it'. On the other hand, if system-imposed tasks are taking up a large chunk of your time and stopping you from achieving your work or life goals, perhaps you could think about delegating them to someone else or hiring someone to do them for you.

Self-imposed time

There are two kinds of self-imposed time: discretionary and subordinate-imposed.

Eighth analysis: Pinpoint discretionary activities

Discretionary time is Proactive time. We choose how we will spend it: on Value-adding activities or on Marginal activities.

With a coloured highlighter, mark each discretionary activity shown on the Make Time Model on page 68 or your Time Log with a symbol such as a dash.

Are you using your discretionary time to do mostly Value-adding tasks and to take an occasional 'on-the-job' break in Quadrant 3? Could you (or should you) spend more discretionary time on Value-adding activities?

What can you do to get more discretionary time for Quadrant 1 (or even Quadrant 3)? If you can't think of at least five things, Part 3 of this book will amply reward you with ideas.

Ninth analysis: Identify the monkeys you can eliminate

Subordinate-imposed time is time taken up by the monkeys we discussed in Chapter 4; that is, activities our team delegates upwards to us.

Take another look at the monkeys you underscored earlier (in the third analysis).

How many can you rid yourself of by putting them back where they belong? If you need help to do this, you will find it in Chapter 14.

Where are you spending the bulk of your time: on boss-imposed tasks, system-imposed tasks, or discretionary tasks? Is the balance right? Could you improve it to achieve your goals more easily? Which Quadrants do they fall into? What does this tell you?

Types of activities

Here is another way to analyse how you are spending your time.

Value-added work

As we've seen, Value-added work is important. Whether it falls in Quadrant 1 or 2, it makes a genuine contribution to achieving results in the Key Result Areas of your working and private lives.

Re-work

This is work you are doing a second or even a third time because it wasn't done right the first time. What a waste of time and effort! Not for nothing do we say:

Do it right first time.

If you think you don't have time to do it right, make sure you have time to do it over!

As the 19th century American poet Henry Wadsworth Longfellow pointed out:

'It takes less time to do something right
than to explain why it was done wrong.'

Non-productive work

This is work that is necessary but not productive in the sense that it doesn't make a genuine contribution to your Key Result Areas. Work of this sort is often system-imposed or boss-imposed. We normally can't do much about it and fortunately, in most jobs, it doesn't represent a large chunk of time.

Unnecessary work

This is work that does no-one—you, your boss, or the system—any good. It often involves tasks we do out of habit or that are leftovers from a previous system. This represents a large waste of time and effort in many people's lives. Identify and eliminate unnecessary work as fast as possible!

Not working

Time spent waiting and sick days are often unavoidable. Holidays and coffee breaks might be avoidable, but we like them! As long as time spent not working does not represent a large chunk of your time, don't worry about reducing it.

Tenth analysis: Spot re-work and unnecessary work

With one of your highlighters, use two other marks, such as a dot point and an X, to highlight activities on your Make Time Model on page 68 or boxes on your Time Log that represent any re-work and unnecessary work that you do. Then decide how you will eliminate both of these time wasters. Be ruthless! How much time can you free up?

The final analysis

Take a look at your Time Logs. What do your earlier ten analyses tell you about how you are using your time? Here are some points to consider:

- Look at the way your time is currently split between the four Quadrants in the Make Time Model, the three types of time Mintzberg identified, and the five types of activities listed above. Where are your problem areas?
- Where are you spending the balance of your time: on boss-imposed tasks, system-imposed tasks, or discretionary tasks? Is the balance right? Could it be improved to make you more effective? Do you have too many monkeys on your back?
- Are you using your discretionary time wisely?
- How many tasks, projects, or other Value-adding activities that you wanted to complete did you actually complete?
- Are there any patterns in the way you use your time or waste your time? Of the Value-adding activities you didn't complete, were there any patterns? For example, were they long and involved activities? Activities involving others? Activities involving a particular type of work? Did you start out enthusiastically and then find your energy petered out?

By now, you know a great deal about how you spend and, perhaps, how you waste your time. Making time hinges on doing what's important. The more Value-adding activities we undertake, the more we will achieve our goals and our personal vision for a balanced life.

The next chapter outlines ten principles to help you make time.

CHOOSE YOUR BATTLES

Grant me the Courage to change the things I can,
The Patience to live with those I can't,
and the Wisdom to know the difference.
About the Patience . . .
I want it *right now!*

Exploring the Make Time principles

Ten principles to help you make time to live your life the way you want to live it

I'M SEARCHING FOR TIME

Have you fallen prey to any of these widespread time management myths?

- Tackle the difficult jobs first.
- Work long hours to show loyalty and commitment.
- I can remember what needs to be done.
- Doing things as they crop up is an efficient way to manage time.
- Deadlines add unnecessary pressure.
- Work on the most urgent matters first.
- Help people when they ask for it.
- If I do my best, things will work out for themselves.

These common myths actually prevent us from managing our time effectively and achieving the things we want to achieve. This chapter will free you from their tyranny.

Principle 1: Know what you want to achieve

Do you know clearly what you want to achieve and by when you want to achieve it? Have you thought about what you want from each facet of your life and are you working steadily towards it? Do you know what lies over the next hurdle?

Unless you can answer 'Yes' to these questions, chances are you're wandering aimlessly through life and your efforts are random, taking you closer towards your goals only by chance. When you run into difficulties you won't have the drive to surmount them. You'll lack a guidepost by which to assess your effectiveness and keep you travelling in the right direction.

It has been said:

If you don't create your own future, someone else will.

Are you willing to leave your future in someone else's hands?

One of the first things racing car drivers learn is what to do when they lose control of their car and go into a spin. People's natural reaction is to focus on the trees they're heading towards, but if we focus there, that's where we'll go. Instead, racing car drivers learn to focus on where they *want* to end up: their destination.

Goals serve the same function for us. They give us something to focus on, guide our efforts, and, if they're clear and compelling enough, draw us towards them like a magnet.

Success has less to do with speed than direction.

In the words of Zig Ziglar, US motivational speaker and author:

*'Success is not a destination. It is a journey. The happiest people
I know are those who are busy working towards specific
objectives. The most bored and miserable people
I know are those who are drifting along with no worthwhile
objectives in mind.'*

The objectives we choose set the tone for our lives and the way we live them. They direct our attention and our efforts and

'The future is not the result
of choices among alternative
paths offered. It is a place that is created.
Created first in mind and will, created next
in activity. The future is not some place we
are going to, but one we are creating.
The paths to it are not found but made
and the activity of making them changes
both the maker and the destination.'

Author unknown

motivate us to look beyond problems. With our sights set firmly on our goals, we can more easily find ways around obstacles.

Knowing what we want to achieve stops us from floundering in the sea of life. Remember these eight powerful words:

If it's to be, it's up to me.

> 'Obstacles are those frightful things we see when we take our eyes off our goals.'
>
> *Henry Ford, 1863–1947*
> *Founder of the Ford Motor Company*

Principle 2: Focus your attention on activities that add value

Are you ever tempted to work on the urgent problems immediately, in the mistaken belief that if you postpone them they will become increasingly difficult to handle?

Occasionally, we should grant something that is urgent the 'right of way' over more Value-adding, non-urgent activities. But as we saw in Chapter 4, automatically attending to something simply because it's urgent is a prescription for pandemonium. It almost guarantees that we will postpone Value-adding activities so long that they eventually become urgent too, propelling us into a fruitless and stressful cycle of crisis management.

Some urgent matters should be done, some should be delegated immediately, and some should be postponed or even ignored. It all depends on how much value doing them will add.

Whenever you're confronted with an urgent matter, evaluate it in terms of both its urgency and importance. Will doing it help you achieve important results? How much value will it add if you attend to it now? Can it wait until later? Should you do it or is it in someone else's province? What would happen if you didn't do it?

Once you've evaluated it, follow the four Ds: deal with it, delegate it, delay it or dump it.

Principle 3: Get a life!

Do you consistently put in considerably more time at work than others in similar positions? Your workload may be heavy for a short period of time, but if you regularly stay behind or take work home after your normal working day, this could indicate poor time management. It could also indicate that you are expecting too much of yourself and striving for exceptionally high achievement. If so, are your expectations realistic? Are they reasonable? Are they impinging unfairly on other areas of your life and causing it to fall out of balance?

Perhaps most of your colleagues put in long hours, and you feel pressured to do the same. This could indicate that you have bought into a toxic organisation culture that expects people to show their loyalty and commitment by 'putting in the hours'. Or is everybody around you overworked because the company is unrealistically expecting too much of everyone? Or perhaps it has downsized so much it has moved from 'lean and mean' to 'anorexic and angry'. If any of these apply, perhaps it's time to find a more reasonable employer and a healthier job!

Principle 4: Think it through, plan it out

Someone once said:

'All things are created twice—first in the mind.'

Do you think you can remember everything you need to do? Perhaps you leave yourself little 'reminder notes' scattered around or peppered through your diary to keep you on track? Maybe you're one of the many who leave work-to-be-done floating around on your desk, thinking you'll remember to attend to it when it falls into your field of vision?

Busy people need a more organised plan of action than any of these approaches. This usually means a To Do list of some sort.

Whether on paper or electronic, To Do lists are one of the most effective tools we can use to make time. A list of things to be done helps us allocate priorities and structure our time so that we complete the most important things. It ensures we won't overlook Value-adding tasks.

Whether daily, weekly or even monthly, some type of plan is essential for effective time management. How often should you prepare a To Do list? This depends on how many things you have to do on any given day. A weekly plan may suffice if you have to remember relatively few things. If your life is more hectic, you may need to make or update your plan every day.

Are you concerned that you'll spend more time preparing your To Do list than getting things done? This can happen if you allow yourself to be caught up in layers of prioritising and pointless subdivision of activities. It can happen if you become so caught up in technology that your electronic diary or taskmaster become ends in themselves.

If you think you're the type of person who is vulnerable to this, use the simple To Do list format suggested in Chapter 9. This will help you prioritise what needs to be done quickly and easily and update it with a minimum of fuss.

Principle 5: Stay focused!

Do you believe that by attending to matters as they arise you are making the most efficient use of your time? The problem with this is that things that add little or no value are just as likely to crop up as things that move us towards our goals. We end up keeping busy but achieving little.

DID YOU KNOW?

The same amount of power that it takes to light a refrigerator bulb can be used by a laser to punch a hole through solid metal? Or to send a beam of light to the moon that can be reflected back to earth?

With more focus on the right areas, we can do anything.

Keep your personal vision and Key Result Areas at the top of your mind and use them to focus on the big picture, a strategic view of what you need to do. Keep your attention and efforts focused on Value-adding activities. To make tomorrow's time management easier, give top priority to activities that will help you accomplish other Value-adding tasks.

Following this principle will benefit you in another way: it will keep you out of the trap of attending to small, simple, tasks that you can 'knock off' quickly, while leaving Value-adding matters undone.

Principle 6: Remember Parkinson's Law

Named after Cyril Northcote Parkinson (1909–1993), Parkinson's Law states:

'Work expands to fill the time available—
as we all make work for one another.'

This suggests two things. First, that setting deadlines is a good idea, provided they don't lead to excessive pressure, which actually prevents you from working well, or to superficial treatment of tasks.

If you're one of those people who does not work well under

pressure, make sure the timetable you set for yourself is realistic. If you're one of those people who think you work best under pressure, avoid the temptation to wait until the last minute before beginning. This will actually reduce your effectiveness. Instead, set yourself a tight and challenging timetable.

SHOULD YOU WATCH THE CLOCK?

In some professions, ignoring the clock may be the best way to use time. If you replace brake linings, you know it takes 17 minutes to do the job on an '86 Holden; but if you're dealing with a customer, or operating on a patient, the amount of time you spend with each depends on a range of factors.

The second thing Parkinson's Law suggests is that we can all too easily fall into the trap of foisting work on others. Because of the first half of the law and because of the 80:20 rule, this work is usually non-Value-adding, or Marginal work that contributes little or nothing to anyone's vision or goals. How much meaningless work goes on in your place of employment or personal life?

The 80:20 rule

Developed by Vilfredo Pareto, a 19th century Italian economist and sociologist, the 80:20 rule as it applies to Making Time indicates that we get 80 per cent of our results from 20 per cent of our efforts. Conversely, it means that 80 per cent of our efforts result in little added value.

What a waste! How much time could you save and how much more could you achieve if you could expand those 20 per centers?

Principle 7: Do like tasks together

Do you attend to matters as they stream across your desk or capture your attention? This is guaranteed to dissipate your energy and effectiveness.

Hopping from one activity to another adds pressure, reduces our efficiency and effectiveness, and increases the likelihood that outside forces, not us, control the way we spend our time.

Two things will help you prevent this from happening:

• Do like tasks together. Try to make your phone calls in one block of time, correspondence in another, and so on. This stops your brain having to chop and change and play mental catch up.
• Do one thing at a time and try to finish it before moving on to something else. Admittedly, it is seldom possible to complete big jobs all in one go. However, this is a good way to get things done, particularly those tasks that do not require considerable time.

Principle 8: Say 'No' to monkeys

Are you that obliging soul everyone relies on to help them out of tight spots? Are you the 'cheerful worker' who lends a hand wherever it's needed? Do you rush around attending to everyone else's affairs and not your own?

If so, you need to learn to say 'No' to tasks that don't belong to you. You need to learn to ignore, postpone, or delegate matters that you need not handle yourself. You need to learn to become comfortable with completing your own Value-adding activities first, before lending a helping hand to others.

Does that sound like the dreaded 'That's not my job' syndrome? Nothing could be further from the truth. 'That's not my job' is about failure to take responsibility, buck passing and laziness. Saying 'No' to monkeys is about focusing your attention and efforts on activities that you are paid to do or are responsible for doing. Saying 'No' to monkeys is about placing responsibility squarely where it belongs. It is about helping others take responsibility for completing tasks that belong to them. It is about achieving what you set out to achieve and, at work, what you are paid to achieve.

Does that sound uncharitable?

Charity begins at home.

Once your own important activities are completed, you will be able to help others wholeheartedly, with no feelings of guilt or remorse about your own chores languishing, waiting to be completed. You will also feel better about achieving your own important goals and leading a more balanced life. You will be less likely to feel pulled in all directions, harassed and stressed, and constantly under pressure to do a million things at once. You will probably feel more energetic and encouraged to achieve even more, and be a nicer person for others, and yourself, to be around.

Warning: Failure to apply Principle 8 is likely to result in doing everyone's work except your own and continual frustration resulting from failing to achieve your own goals.

Principle 9: Work in your 'prime time'

We each have our own 'best' time during the day when we should tackle our most difficult tasks. For some, it's early in the morning. For others, it's the afternoon. Others work best in the evenings. What did your fifth analysis of your Time Log tell you about your energy levels? Take maximum advantage of your own periods of peak energy when you plan out your day.

If you're a morning person who wilts in the afternoon, make sure you schedule important activities early in the morning when you're at your best. Schedule important presentations, critical meetings, projects and decisions that need careful thought for the early part of the day. If you must schedule an important meeting or presentation later in the day, have a high protein lunch, eat a piece of fruit, and get some fresh air to energise your body.

Do you hit your stride later in the day? That's when you should schedule your important activities. If you need to have an early start to the day, make sure you can hit the decks running by organising everything thoroughly the night before. Take the time to eat a high protein breakfast or some fruit and get some fresh air.

Principle 10: Prioritise, prioritise, prioritise!

All time management decisions boil down to decisions about priorities. Should you decide to give high priority to small tasks that can be accomplished quickly? To whatever is at the top of your in-tray? To the 'squeaky wheel' or whatever interrupts you? No!

Consciously decide what to do and what not to do based on your priorities. Decide which interruptions to accept and which to reject, what to do now and what to postpone until later, based on your priorities. What should you accord the highest priority? Give high priority to tasks that will add the most value based on your personal vision and Key Result Areas.

Arrange your decisions, tasks and projects into priority order and, as far as possible, work through them in that order. Realistically, of course, interruptions, delays, etc will prevent you from working your way straight through your priority

'Time is the coin of your life. It is the only coin you have and only you can determine how it will be spent. Be careful lest you let other people spend it for you.'

Carl Sandburg, 1878–1967
US author

86

list. Nevertheless, Principle 10 is good to follow because it helps you concentrate on results, not on being busy. It also means that anything you don't complete will have a low priority.

Congratulations!

Now that you have completed Part 2, you know what tasks and activities you need to focus on to achieve the best, and most rewarding, results. You can manage your time effectively.

In Part 3 we look at how to manage your time efficiently. You will discover how to work smarter, not harder.

How to become more efficient

'The great dividing line between success and failure can be expressed in five words: "I did not have time."'

Franklin Field

Identify your time management problem areas

CHAPTER 8

Pinpoint your specific time management headaches

Research by the British Institute of Management tracking more than 5000 managers over a five-year period found that most of them felt under constant time pressure. Eighty per cent, for example, named tight deadlines as the cause of working long hours and over half said they suffer from information overload. Although there is no comparable Australian research, it is reasonable to assume most Australian managers, and perhaps Australians in general, feel the same way.

The research highlights that we need to spot our time management problems and manage them well to survive today's fast-paced environment. The top ten items on the British Institute of Management's 'pressure-ometer' are:

1. constant interruptions

2. time pressure and deadlines

3. poor internal communications

4. lack of support

5. poor senior management

6. too many internal meetings

7. office politics

8. handling change

9. securing the right information

10. keeping up with e-mails.

At least half of these show a clear need for making time.

What are your pressure areas? Do you have lots of interruptions and distractions during your day too? Do you have too much to do and not enough time to do it in? Do you have important, Value-adding jobs waiting to be attended to but you just can't seem to get started? If only you could remove the interruptions and your other time wasters, you would have more time for your Value-adding stuff! It would be easy to get through your To Do list and achieve results!

Here's the bad news: you probably have to learn to live with a lot of your time wasters.

Here's the good news: you can learn to handle them better and gain more discretionary time and time for your Value-adding tasks.

Handling your time wasters better will help you make more productive use of your time. It will free up time to attend to the important things in your life, including time out for relaxing and 'doing nothing' if you need it!

First, you need to identify your personal 'time wasters'. Then you can take steps to minimise or eliminate them.

Identify your biggest time wasters

Review the list of typical time management headaches on the next page and rate yourself on how well you control them. (If you would like to add one or two of your own, do so at the bottom of the list.)

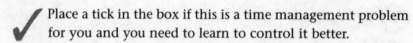 Place a tick in the box if this is a time management problem for you and you need to learn to control it better.

Once you've identified the things that interfere most with your efficiency, target the relevant chapters in this section to find out how to deal with them.

A problem I need to control better	TIME MANAGEMENT PROBLEM	A problem I need to control better	TIME MANAGEMENT PROBLEM
☐	Procrastination	☐	Other people's mistakes
☐	Lack of organisation	☐	Unrealistic objectives
☐	Misplaced items	☐	Negative attitudes
☐	Interruptions	☐	Understaffed
☐	Waiting for work	☐	Poor internal communications
☐	Excessive attention to detail	☐	Wrong choice of priorities
☐	Unnecessary work	☐	Equipment failure
☐	My manager	☐	Allowing diversions
☐	My staff	☐	Trying to do too many things at once
☐	My colleagues, family, or friends	☐	Excessive record keeping
☐	Meetings without goals	☐	Different value systems to organisation or associates, family or friends
☐	Inability to say 'No'	☐	Lack of feedback
☐	Failure to listen	☐	Handling paperwork
☐	Unclear goals and objectives	☐	Inaccurate or incomplete information
☐	Poor delegation	☐	Making a slow start to the day
☐	Socialising	☐	Perfectionism
☐	Using telephone for personal reasons	☐	Messy desk or work area
☐	General tiredness	☐	Too many meetings
☐	Telephone interruptions	☐	Playing computer games
☐	Crisis situations	☐	Distractions, eg noise
☐	Time pressures and deadlines	☐	Untrained staff
☐	Feeling pulled in all directions	☐	Jobs taking longer than they should
☐	Over-committed to activities	☐	Leaving things until the last minute, always rushing
☐	Too much wasted time	☐	Not feeling in control, feeling overwhelmed
☐	Not knowing where or how to make a start	☐	Trying to do everything myself

93

'Unlike other resources,
time cannot be bought or sold,
borrowed or stolen, stocked up or
saved, manufactured, reproduced,
or modified. All we can do is make
use of it. And whether we use it or
not, it nevertheless slips away.'

Jean-Louis Servan-Schreiber, writer

To learn how to make better use of this unique resource, browse through chapters 9–17. Concentrate on the chapters that deal with your most problematic time wasters. Be on the lookout for ideas that will help you eliminate, control or minimise them to make time to do Value-adding things. **Circle or highlight those that seem to hold promise.**

'If you want to get a
good idea, get lots
of ideas.'

Linus Pauling, 1901–1994
US chemist and Nobel Prize winner

Do you recognise any of these tips and ideas? If so, ask yourself: 'what has been preventing me from applying them?'

CHAPTER 9

Think it through, plan it out

The ABCs of time management

I'VE LOST MY PRIORITY LIST!

Do you ever get really busy and worry that you'll never get everything done? Let's face it—few us are always going to get everything done.

This is why it's important to make sure that what does get done adds value and that anything left undone is mundane and Marginal. How? Through planning. As the saying goes:

Prior planning prevents poor performance.

With enough focus on the right things, lack of time will be a thing of the past. To Do lists are our primary tool to help us plan how we will use our time and do the things we really want to do. They show us what to focus on: our Value-adding tasks, responsibilities, and duties. They help us choose what to do and what to leave until later. They help us stay 'on top of things' and protect us from chaos and whim.

To Do lists also help us track our commitments. Broken promises, to ourselves or to others, cost us our self-respect and the respect of those we've let down. They weaken relationships, both at work and at home. And on the other side of the coin, To Do lists can remind us not to let others forget their commitments to us.

Create a To Do list

Try making a daily or weekly To Do list. For work, use your Key Result Areas (see Chapter 5) to guide you. For home, use the goals you have set yourself as a guide (see Chapters 2 and 5). Some people prefer to have one To Do list for home and one for work; others prefer to combine them. Try both ways and stick with the one that works best for you.

Some people use their diaries as their To Do lists. Others prefer electronic task managers or paper-based lists. Whichever you use, don't let your organiser become an end in itself! It's a tool to help you manage your time, nothing more.

You'll see a sample of a simple paper-based To Do list combined with a telephone record summary on page 98. It uses an A-4 size spiral-bound notebook. On one side is the To Do list and on the other, the telephone record summary. Try it: you'll find the To Do list part works really well once you've worked out which categories are best for you.

The telephone record can be a lifesaver, too, because you have a readily available record of all your phone calls showing the date, who you spoke to and what was agreed. (If your job is more about informal meetings than telephone calls, it might be better to make the telephone summary pages summaries of informal meetings in your office instead.) Every time you use the phone or conclude a meeting, just note down who you spoke to or met with, what was concluded, and who agreed to do what. Then transfer anything you need over to your To Do list.

'He who every morning plans the transaction of the day and follows out that plan, carries a thread that will guide him through the maze of the most busy life. But where no plan is laid, where the disposal of time is surrendered merely to the chance of incidence, chaos will soon reign.'

Victor Hugo, 1802–1885
French poet, novelist, and dramatist

TO DO LIST

(date)

PHONE

A Sam Confirm meeting
    Progress on Smith account?
    Month end figures
A Lee—Board proposal—any changes
B Ann—update—vacant position
C Charlie Proof report?
    Jim? Meeting
    Latest figures
C Nickie Confirm lunch
    Document received?
B Bank—query automatic withdrawal
A Geoff—re Feb.

MEETINGS—APPOINTMENTS

Cindy—performance appraisal
    3 pm Wednesday
Production mtg—11 am Wed.
Thursday—dentist—2 pm
Joanne—exit interview, Mon. 10 am
Nola—Tues. 8 am—progress report

WRITE

B Agenda for Super's meeting
B Update on training plan
A Bard—cover letter—proposal
C Quarterly progress report
B Expenses
B Scott—send article
B Paul—send article
C John—update—Email

FOLLOW-UP

C Jane—get back to me re invoice
B Bob—still OK for Fri?
A Payment due from Smith & Co—
    received?
A Job ad ready?
B Stats for overtime
C James—Bliss report
C Peter—Council regulations?
A Sue—keys

MISC

A Gather figures for production meeting
A Prepare for Cindy's performance appraisal
B Clear filing backlog!

TELEPHONE RECORD

11/10
Jan D—she'll get amended contract
    to me by Friday

11/10
Sam—OK for Fri. He'll pick me up.

11/10
Nadia—Dyson report. She'll do
agenda & fax for approval by Thurs.

11/10
Ben—apologies for Wed. meeting
⇨ Add to apologies list.

11/10
Fred—can I help with proofing proposal? Only if he gets it to me by Mon. week.
Fred to follow up.

12/10
Don—needs report to include: 1) last
month's stats; 2) bar chart of year-
to-date; 3) Recommendations in bullet
point form.
⇨ Amend as agreed

12/10
Chen—meet to discuss IT project.
⇨ Me to bring list of my wants &
    needs. Next Tues?
⇨ Confirm on Friday.

12/10
Robyn—dinner on Sat?
She'll make reservation & confirm back.

12/10
Steph—me to send revised workbook
this week.
⇨ UPDATE!

13/10
Jan—problems with contract.
New date—Wed. week.

HOW TO MAKE
A GREAT TO DO LIST

1. Buy an A4 sized spiral pad and fold it back so only one side sits open. The 'main page' is for your To Do list. The 'reverse page' is to summarise your telephone calls or informal meetings at your desk.

2. Select four or five categories that represent main chunks of your time. Divide the To Do list page into four or five sections and label each section with one of your chosen categories.

3. Date the To Do list at the top.

4. List your tasks under their appropriate categories. If you have a lot of items to get through, prioritise them using the ABC system (explained on page 102).

5. Add tasks to your To Do list throughout the day as they crop up, prioritising as appropriate. Keep what you write brief—just enough so that you can easily recall what is needed.

6. As you complete a task, cross it out.

7. When your To Do list becomes too messy to live with, begin a new one. Turn the page, date it, and set it up with your categories. Transfer over items that you haven't completed and you will have a new, tidy To Do list to work from.

8. If you find you are re-writing a task three or more times, question whether you really need to do it at all. If you don't, dump it. If you do, what's stopping you? Do what you have to do to complete the item, and cross it off your list.

You are likely to find at first that items that keep shifting across onto new To Do lists are Value-adding but not urgent, so they're easy to skip over. Re-writing them several times will cause you to question them. If they are Value-adding, you know how important it is to allocate time to do them. So do it!

Play around with the categories you use on your paper or electronic To Do lists. You might want to make 'commitments', for example, a special category on your paper list, or a subcategory on your computer task list.

When you write down things you want to do, keep your comments brief: the list is for you, no-one else, and you'll know what you're referring to. For example, if you need to meet with Fred to discuss the latest customer retention figures and brainstorm some ways to improve customer relations, you might only need to write 'Fred—retention figures and customer relations'. See the sample To Do list on page 98.

Every day, review your To Do list as often as necessary to make sure you are honouring your obligations to yourself and others and doing the most important Value-adding activities. If you aren't going to be able to keep a commitment, telephone the person affected, explain what has happened to prevent you from honouring it, and re-schedule.

Schedule some work time to attend to home-related matters and vice versa. Keeping our personal and professional lives separate causes stress, so integrate them when you can.

If there is a lot on your To Do list, set priorities for each item based on what is important. Making time is about our personal priorities and what adds the most value to our lives.

> *Think it through.*
> *Plan it out.*

Setting priorities

Whatever we do, or don't do, time will move ahead at one second per second. We have no power over time, but we do have power over how we use it. To use it well, we need to know our priorities— what is important and what isn't. That takes us straight back to our goals (see Chapters 2 and 5).

Do you operate a To Do list but without much success? Perhaps it isn't helping you establish your priorities and focus on them. Or perhaps there is so much on it, it's more confusing and daunting than helpful! Try using the ABC system, outlined on the next page, for three weeks and see if things improve.

The ABC priority system

Write a capital letter 'A' to the left of those tasks that are highest priority; a 'B' for those with medium priority; and a 'C' for those with low priority. (Try selecting the 'A's first, then the 'C's, and everything left is a 'B'.)

By comparing each item on your list with the others and against your goals and Key Result Areas, you will be able to come up with sound ABC priority choices for every item on your list. You are the best judge of your own priorities and as long as you focus them around your KRAs, you will reap the rewards of Making Time.

'A' items should be those that give the most value in terms of your Key Result Areas. They are the major things you want to accomplish. You'll make best use of your time by doing the 'A's first and saving the 'B's and 'C's for later.

Most 'B's and 'C's will eventually become 'A's if you don't attend to them. If they don't, it could mean they don't need to be done at all.

Your ABC priorities may change over time, so stay flexible and focused on the best use of your time *right now*.

Remember Victor Hugo's words: 'When the disposal of time is surrendered to the chance of incidents, chaos will reign.'

Plan each day and set priorities. Start with the 'A' items and work your way down. Feel the success each time you complete and cross an item off your list!

*What's the best use of your time **right now**?*

GOOD ADVICE

Ivy Lee, often called the founder of management consulting, advised Charles Schwab, then president of Bethlehem Steel Corporation in the USA: 'Number the items you have to do tomorrow in the order of their real importance. First thing tomorrow morning, start working on number one and stay with it until it is completed. Next take number two and don't go any further until it, too, is completed. Then proceed to number three, and so on. If you can't complete everything on the day's schedule, don't worry. At least you'll have taken care of the most important things without getting distracted by items of lesser importance.'

Lee asked Schwab to test the system and pay him whatever it was worth. A few weeks later, Schwab sent Lee a cheque for US$25,000 (worth more than 20 times as much today).

The moral of the story?

Prioritise your tasks and deal with them one by one.

Don't just stop at prioritising! Do whatever you have to do to make sure you devote time to your high priority activities. For example:

- Schedule them into your diary.
- Begin and end the workday by devoting a block of time to a high priority activity.
- Devote your prime time to high priority activities.
- Devote time when you get up in the mornings and come home from work to important personal and family goals.
- Allocate time on weekends and/or days off to reaching your goals for achieving a balanced life.

Some reasons why time plans may not work

If you find it nearly impossible to complete everything on your To Do list each day, you're in good company. The important thing is that you accomplish your top, or 'A', priorities.

If you are able to complete only a few things on your To Do list and find yourself leaving the majority undone, though, you need some help! Perhaps you are having trouble completing your list each day for one or more of the following reasons:

- Are you trying to accomplish too much? Perhaps you have an impractical number of items on your personal or work To Do list or you are setting unrealistically high standards for yourself.

- Are you avoiding doing some of the things on your list for some reason?

- Are your goals fuzzy?

- Are you jumping into a task in the middle without sufficiently analysing it step by step and 'spinning your wheels' as a result?

- Are you ignoring your priorities?

- Are you attending to 'squeaky wheel' Marginal tasks while leaving Value-adding tasks undone?

- Do you avoid making decisions?

- Due to a breakdown in communication, could it be that you don't have all the information you need to complete things?

- Is your self-discipline failing you? Do you do whatever is easiest, most enjoyable, quickest, or at the top of the pile?

- Are you feeling too pressured to stop and catch your breath and think things through and plan them out?

- Are you not staying with tasks because you find them difficult or boring, or because of too many interruptions?

- Are you carrying around other peoples monkeys because you're reluctant to say 'No'?

- Are you less than fully committed to achieving the tasks on your list?

- Do you lack the self-confidence to tackle the more difficult jobs?

- Are you testing the water around the edges of a task instead of plunging in?

- Are you dwelling on past failures instead of working towards future success?

- Are you thinking: 'I probably won't finish it' instead of 'I can and I will get this done!'?
- Does a hectic environment or the need for a lot of 'troubleshooting' make planning difficult?
- Do you tend to put things off until the deadline looms?

For many of us, there is never enough time to do all the things we want to do and need to do. We must choose between competing demands on our time. The choices we make mean that we, at the end of the day, are responsible for how we spent our time, how much we achieved and, ultimately, how stressed and fatigued we feel. Use a prioritised To Do list to help you focus on, and achieve, the most important things in *your* life.

> 'Don't tell me how hard you work; tell me how much you get done.'
>
> *James Ling*

Tips for team leaders

If you have a team of people reporting to you, you can help them set and achieve goals. Try holding a weekly meeting, either at the beginning or the end of the week. Each team member brings their Goal Sheet or To Do list with 'A' priorities marked. This is what they want to achieve for the week.

Each has five minutes to share their goals, either work-related only or both work and personal. Team members can challenge each other: Are your goals realistic? Are they challenging enough?

The entire meeting shouldn't take more than about 20 minutes and the benefits will far outweigh the time spent. Stating one's goals publicly increases commitment and is motivating: the pressure is on to achieve! Prioritising like this increases productivity and reduces crises. These meetings strengthen the team and, because they know each other's goals, team members can help each other stay focused on them.

Try this at the family dinner table, too! At the beginning or the end of the week, talk about what each of you wants to achieve during the coming week. Then you'll be able to support each other or, at least, not stand in each other's way.

CHAPTER **10**

Expand your efficiency

Work smarter not harder

It has been said that efficiency is intelligent laziness. Intelligent it certainly is, but hopefully not laziness! Being efficient means doing things in 'smart' ways that shave off seconds, eliminate wasted mental and physical effort, and streamline and make the most of your efforts.

Some general tips

- Prepare a list of 'Musts' (top priorities) to accomplish each day.

- Review your list throughout the day to determine whether you need to adjust the way you are using your time.

- Don't hop from one thing to another. Wherever possible, group similar activities and tasks together and reserve a block of time to work on them. For example, make your outgoing phone calls in one block of time, then spend some time filing, then put in some serious effort on a project. This saves you constantly switching 'mental gears' and streamlines your efforts.

- Prepare a daily plan and work to it.

- Take enough time to do it right first time, so you don't need to do it over.

- Delegate more tasks and projects that can be delegated.

- Devote more time to training and developing people's skills so that they can help you out.

- Use the delegation plan in Chapter 14 and decide how others can relieve some of the pressure.

- If you can't finish a job now, try to break at a natural stopping point. Make a note to yourself on undeveloped thoughts and what you want to do next.

- Save unimportant and non-urgent tasks for when you have a few minutes of slack time or want a quick mental break.

- Work on one thing at a time. Remove non-immediate work from your field of vision.

- Use the Swiss Cheese technique for big jobs: break them up into smaller tasks and make a start!

- Continually ask: 'What is the best use of my time *right now*?' especially when you are feeling overwhelmed with how much needs to be done.

- Develop positive self-talk to lower your stress. Instead of saying 'I'll never get through all this', say 'I'll take one thing at a time and get it done bit by bit.'

- Let others know what your priorities are. They may find ways to help you achieve them that you wouldn't have thought of yourself.

- Beware of the 'We've always done it this way' syndrome. Analyse tasks, particularly routine and recurring administrative matters. If there is not a safety reason for a particular method, could you streamline it? How else could you do it to increase efficiency and save time?

- Carry an Ideas Notebook. Jot down things you want to remember, promises you have made, good ideas that pop into your mind. Review it at least weekly and act on what you've written.

- Identify your most productive period of the day and use that time for your most demanding tasks.

- Stay fresh by changing 'tempo' regularly; at least every hour to 90 minutes.

- Some small tasks may not need to be completed to perfection and some do not need to be completed at all. Learn to recognise tasks you are *over-completing*; that is, spending too much time on. Don't spend too much time for too few results.

- Develop your technical skills. Spending even five or ten minutes learning one new thing every day (for example, how to organise your computer files, how to use more functions on your electronic time organiser) can help improve your efficiency and productivity by 60 per cent. Invest time to save time!

- If a time management technique works at work, try it at home, and vice versa.

- Think in your prime time, do in your down time.

- Work to your strengths. As Ingas Bernstein said: 'If you're a runner, run; if you're a bell, ring.'

- Enjoy what you're doing. The great inventor, Thomas Edison, was oblivious to time's passing once he began an experiment. When someone asked him the secret of his success, he said: 'Don't look at your watch.'

  If you look at your watch a lot, it indicates you're not engrossed in what you're doing. Should you be doing something else that you would relish doing more?

- Do it *now*!

Get organised!

Are you a natural born slob? Do you often forget to do things? Have you forgotten what the top of your desk looks like? The only way you will be able to get yourself organised, get things done in a non-chaotic and timely fashion, and . . . yes . . . stop annoying those around you, will be to become more organised.

Don't take the easy way out and see your chronic disorganisation as a personality flaw you can't change. Disorganisation is a habit and you can change it if you persist.

Or perhaps you believe you work best in 'organised chaos'? Some people do. Ask yourself these five questions:

1 Do I ever spend time looking for staplers, paper clips, files or computer discs with information on them that I need?

2 Do I spend time looking for documents that I use often?

3 Do I ever experience mild panic when I can't find an important file?

4 Do I ever become exasperated when something has 'gone missing?'

5 Do I often forget to follow things up and leave tasks unfinished?

If you can answer 'Yes' to any of these questions, you need to improve your personal organisation. The messier you are, the more commitment you will need. You probably have years of bad habits to break! However, if you put in the effort required to develop the good time management habits suggested below, you will be glad you did.

> 'Don't agonise—
> organise!'
> *Florynce Kennedy*

Perfect your personal organisation and planning

As you read through the following list, select three things to start doing *now* to improve your personal organisation.

- Adopt this motto: 'A place for everything and everything in its place.' Make sure everything you use has a *place*. Discipline yourself to put things back in their *place* as soon as you've finished using them. Don't put off putting them away until later. You probably won't get around to it and will become overwhelmed by the mess surrounding you!

- Organise your desk. Keep the active files, current projects, and forms and documents that you use regularly close to hand. The filing drawer of your desk is ideal. Use it fanatically. When you aren't working on it *right now*—file it away! Even if you plan to work on it later—*file it away!*

- The same goes for stationery items. Put your stapler, paper clips, spare computer discs—everything you use regularly—away (in the same place each time) and easily accessible. When you've finished using something, *put it back!* When you aren't using it—*put it away!* Even if you know you'll be using it later—*put it away!* This will keep your work area tidy. You'll spend less time searching for things and feel less stressed and more in control.

- Searching for things eats up precious minutes and increases your stress level. Putting things away takes seconds and saves you both time and stress.

- If important items that you always need 'mysteriously disappear', keep them in a secret place that only you know about. Nothing is more frustrating than having to search for basic essentials when you're short of time.

- Keep it clear! Remove non-immediate work from your field of vision. *Put it away if you aren't using it right now!* The bigger a slob you are, the more fanatical you *must* be about this!

- Do one thing at a time! If you try to do too many things at once, you end up not doing any very well. For most of us, 'multi-tasking' means 'messing up several things at once'.

- Avoid the fatigue and mistakes that occur from a last-minute rush to reach a poorly planned deadline or to complete something you've left until the last minute. The larger the project, the more you should divide it into action steps, each with a target completion date. Keep track of what needs to be done on your To Do list. Develop your plan and stick to it.

- Keep notes of ideas, conversations, commitments and decisions. That way, you won't forget them or waste time re-inventing the wheel.

- Don't kid yourself with 'busy work' rather than productive work. You can do 'C' priorities and no-one can say you aren't working, but you'll still be avoiding your most Value-adding jobs. You might even be working efficiently, but you won't be working effectively!

- Stay fresh by changing 'tempo' regularly, at least every hour to 90 minutes.

- Change your mindset. Do things because you *want to* do them (not because you *have to*). This subtle change of wording helps you approach tasks whole-heartedly and achieve much better results.

- Save Marginal and non-urgent tasks for when you have a few minutes of slack time or want a mental break.

- Work in your 'prime time'. Identify your most productive periods of the day and use these times for your most demanding tasks.

- Don't try to increase your energy with chocolate bars or caffeine (coffee, soft drinks or 'energy' drinks). If you need an energy boost, eat some protein or fruit and get some fresh air.

- Carry an Ideas Notebook with you to jot down good ideas, reminders to yourself, promises you've made. This is a great memory aid: it takes a load off your brain! Go through your Ideas Notebook regularly and act on what you've written.

- Know what's really important in your personal life as well as your work life. If you spend all your time achieving 'A' priorities at work but fail to achieve them in your personal life, you'll feel stressed and dissatisfied.

- Develop positive self-talk to lower your stress. Instead of saying 'I'll never get through all this', say 'I'll take one thing at a time and get it done bit by bit.'

- Don't clutter up your space with bits of paper or sticky notes. Write important information wherever it belongs: in your contact database, diary, task manager, or the relevant file.

- Make it easy to do things. For instance, keep stationery for business and private correspondence close to hand and your address book or contact list nearby. When the time comes to write a note, it's easier to sit down and write it because you won't have to go hunting for the supplies.

- Have a junk file for things like junk mail, For Your Information memos, etc. Go through it when you have nothing better to do or when you need a break. Or carry the file when you're travelling and go through it in your down time.

Use your diary

The diary, whether paper-based or electronic, is one of our most important tools for making time. Used well, it will be your road map to coordinating your life and staying on track to achieve your goals. Use it to manage both your work life and your personal life.

- List all your appointments and contact details in it.
- List all your important tasks in it.

- Block out chunks of time to attend to your most important, Value-adding tasks.

- When you make appointments in your diary or electronic scheduler, note down contact details (telephone number and address) in case you are running behind and need to telephone them. This will save last-minute panics about where to find them.

- Put in reminders before an important event to alert you to prepare for it.

- Try an electronic diary if you haven't already. It can beep to remind you to complete tasks and keep appointments. (If you want to be reminded again, hit 'snooze'.)

- Try a virtual calendar (for example, MS Outlook). A virtual calendar allows you to e-mail appointments for others to click straight into their diaries.

- Look at your diary every day to make sure you don't miss anything.

Follow through and follow up faithfully

Some people consistently honour their commitments. If they say they'll telephone you in two weeks time to discuss something, they do it. Do they have a brain that never forgets anything? Possibly, but more likely they operate a reliable follow-up system.

- Whenever you do something that needs to be followed up (sending a brochure or proposal, seeing how someone is proceeding with a delegated task, etc) note this down on your follow-up list. This could be a separate list, a section of your To Do list or electronic task manager, or a simple electronic or paper 'bring forward' filing system.

- The same applies when someone makes a commitment to you. Have people agreed to keep you posted on the 20th of every month or to send you some information? Note this down on your follow up list. If they don't contact you, contact them: they'll soon learn you expect them to honour their commitment.

- Whenever you make a commitment, for example, to telephone someone or send something, note this down in your Ideas

Notebook (if you are away from your desk) or your To Do list. Follow it through and don't cross it off until you've done it.

- When noting things to follow up or follow through, make brief notes about the person, his/her contact details and what you'll be following up or following through. This will make life easier for you when the time comes to act.

- The above applies to your personal, as well as your professional, life. Sometimes, if we don't note down our desire to keep in touch with family or friends, time passes without the intended contact and the relationship withers. Keeping in touch is important in all facets of our life.

Tips for team leaders

Do people wanting to speak to you create constant interruptions? Do informal 'meetings' ruin your train of thought, break into your thinking time and concentration, and destroy your ability to plan your day? Think about making up a Meet File for each person you interact with regularly: your boss, your staff, your colleagues. That way, you won't constantly interrupt each other for short durations. You can save things up and cover several points together, which will make your meetings more effective.

People often want instant responses, but often there is no urgency attached. Get into the habit, and get your team into the habit, of saving things up for a convenient time for everyone.

File a manila folder with each person's name on it and keep it in an easily

'To have an uncluttered mind at the end of each day, make a list of everything, even the little things, that you must accomplish the next day. Then, make sure you end that day with a clean slate.'

Benjamin Franklin, 1706–1790
US statesman, writer and scientist

accessible place. When something crops up that you want to discuss or draw to their attention, note it down in their folder. Go through the folder each time you meet to keep up-to-date.

Conquer chaos: Turn havoc into harmony

Do you sometimes feel you're sitting in the middle of a disaster area? If the previous section didn't offer enough suggestions for creating calmness out of commotion, here are some more.

'A life lived in chaos is an impossibility.'

Madeleine L'Engle, 1918–
Science fiction novelist

- Stop and think. How should you handle the tasks you need to do? How can you work best with others involved in those tasks? How can you involve others in what you need to do to take some of the pressure off?

- Eliminate noise. Noise causes misinterpreted messages, disrupts thought and adds to confusion and tension.

- Listen. Take time to listen to yourself and the people around you. Listen and look for verbal and non-verbal messages.

- When a mountain of work faces you, ask yourself: 'What will contribute most to my personal vision or job goals? Which, if done today, will help me add value tomorrow?'

- Ask yourself: 'Why am I overloaded? What role do I have in this chaos? Who else might my actions be affecting? How do I want things to be?'

God did not create hurry.

Finnish proverb

116

STRESSING OUT?

Breathe. Three deep breaths will start the oxygen flowing to your neocortex, your 'Thinking Brain'. When we're stressed, rushed, harried and harassed, we tend to breathe shallowly and oxygen, which we need to think, deserts our Thinking Brain and heads south to our Emotional Brain. We can't think straight.

Three deep breaths will help clear your mind and help you regain your perspective. The increased flow of oxygen to your brain (and heart) will help calm you, sooth you, and reduce your anxiety. It will help you think more clearly and creatively.

Purge procrastination! Get started on those jobs you love to put off

If Robert Benchley's quote is true for you, here are some tips to help you get started.

- Commit to a firm deadline.
- Try setting *start* (instead of finish) deadlines.
- Plan tomorrow, but *do* today.
- Slice projects and large time-consuming tasks into smaller, more manageable chunks, or specific To Do steps. Set start dates for each step and get started! Put a deadline on each step and stick to it.

'Anyone can do any amount of work provided it isn't the work he is supposed to be doing at the moment.'

Robert Benchley, 1889–1945
Humorist, drama critic and actor

In the words of the US writer and philosopher Ralph Waldo Emerson:

'The creation of a thousand forests is in one acorn.'

• Divide a large task into smaller subtasks and work on them one at a time until the whole task is complete. This is amazingly effective. Completing bite size chunks quickly adds up.

'The secret of getting ahead is getting started. The secret of getting started is breaking your complex overwhelming tasks into small manageable tasks, and then starting on the first one.'

Mark Twain, 1835–1910
US author and humorist

• Reward yourself with a break or change of pace after completing a task.

• Talk it through with others. Even if they don't have your experience or skill, they may say something that gives you the inspiration you need.

• Stuck? Find the real problem. Do you need more information? Different information? Input from someone else? What is your stumbling block? How can you remove it or go around it?

• Do the least desirable tasks first if they're important, and get them out of the way so they won't be hanging over your head like the sword of Damocles.

- Don't put off Value-adding but unpleasant tasks: this will block your brain and reduce your creativity and work capacity. (But do put off everything that does not add value so that you can focus on things that directly contribute to your effectiveness.)

> 'When you have a number of disagreeable duties to perform, always do the most disagreeable first.'
> *Josiah Quincy, 1744–1775*
> *US lawyer*

- Apply the 'must—should—could' test to every task. Spend most of your time on 'must' items, get to 'shoulds' as soon as you can, and stop worrying about 'coulds'.
- If a task must be done, do it *now* and get it out of the way!

Or as Ben Franklin said:

> *'You may delay, but time will not.'*

> 'Procrastination is the thief of time.'
> *Edward Young, 1683–1765*
> *English poet*

- Unless you're already working silly hours, start work half an hour earlier.
- If you don't have enough information, get it.
- Start the day doing a Value-adding task, not a Marginal one. (Is checking the e-mail *really* important?)
- Make time in your schedule to do the tasks you usually avoid and honour your commitment to yourself to attend to them.
- At the end of the day, clear your desk. This will give you a fresh start the next morning.
- Set aside as much time as you'll need to clear your desk of outstanding work. Don't

> 'Hard work is often the easy work you did not do at the proper time.'
> *Bernard Meltzer*

'Only put off until tomorrow what you are willing to die having left undone.'

Pablo Picasso, 1881–1974
Spanish artist

even answer the telephone until you've done it.

• Are you getting stuck on the minor details? If so, re-focus. Let the minor things wait until the major ones are completed.

'Know the true value of time; snatch, seize, and enjoy every moment of it. No idleness; no laziness; no procrastination. Never put off until tomorrow what you can do today.'

Philip Stanhope, 4th Earl of Chesterfield, 1694–1773
English politician and author

CHAPTER **11** # Influence interruptions

Defeat those disturbances!

RING
RING

'It is difficult to produce a television documentary that is both incisive and probing when every 12 minutes one is interrupted by 12 dancing rabbits singing about toilet paper.'

Rod Serling, 1924–1975
Actor, producer, and screenwriter

Do you get your work done in the intermissions between interruptions? Just when you're making some headway, the phone rings. Just when you're about to finish off something complicated, someone disrupts your thoughts and asks if you can spare a minute. Just when you're about to capture that fleeting, but great idea, an incoming e-mail snatches your concentration. Is there any way around this?

In time management terms, interruptions can be deadly. People in busy offices get interrupted, on average, once every eight or nine minutes. For some people, interruptions, whether from customers or internal people, are an important part of their job. For others, interruptions intrude and irritate. Take heart: you can curb those disturbances.

Some general tips

Professor Robert Kelley of Carnegie-Mellon's Graduate School of Industrial Administration, who has researched the difference between high and low performing employees, says a major cause of poor performance is frequent interruptions. With brain-powered work, he says, the hard part is getting into the flow of thought.

He likens it to launching a spaceship: breaking out of the earth's atmosphere uses more fuel and creates more stress than any other part of the trip; once in space, movement sustains itself. When we're interrupted, we lose momentum and must 'launch' ourselves all over again.

He suggests some ways to create work space to prevent interruptions:

- Put on a pair of headphones while you work. People will be reluctant to interrupt.
- Find a quiet place where you can work without interruption; for example, an empty office or conference room. Before you disappear, though, let people know where you'll be.
- Shut your door and post a visitor's list for people to sign, with a second column to list what they want to see you about. This will also help you prepare for when you do meet with them.

Here are some other tips to try:

- Decide whether the interruption is part of your job or not and deal with it accordingly.
- When someone interrupts you, they make their priority your priority. Sometimes, it's important to deal with an interruption immediately. Sometimes, it isn't. Make a conscious decision about when to deal with the interruption. If possible, schedule a more convenient time.
- If you must deal with the interruption and finish what you were working on later, try to break at a natural stopping point. Take a moment to make a note to yourself about what you were doing and what remains to be done. Then take a deep breath and give the person your full concentration and attention. When you're finished, your note will remind you of what to carry on with.
- If you think the interruption will take less than half an hour and you decide to deal with it now, once you've dealt with it try to get straight back to what you were doing before the interruption.
- If you think the interruption will take longer than half an hour, do these three things:
  1. Make a note of what your next step should be on what you were doing.
  2. Close up the file you were working on and put it away.
  3. Make a note on your To Do list to get back to it.
- Screen interruptions carefully to avoid every interruption you can.

- Close the door when you don't want interruptions.
- Arrange for a 'quiet time': one or two hours when those sharing the office do not interrupt each other. Diarise it as 'meeting with yourself', 'quiet time', 'quality time', or 'planning time'. Prevent as many external interruptions as possible during the quiet time, too; for example, by diverting your phone or switching to voice mail, moving into a meeting or conference room, getting in half an hour earlier than usual, and telling team members that you need some uninterrupted planning or project time.

> Management guru Peter Drucker says that 90 minutes of uninterrupted time is equivalent to four hours of interrupted time. Most of us can't get this much time unless we block it out in our diary and make arrangements to prevent interruptions. Clearly, the effort required to do this is worth it.

Tame the telephone

Does your telephone ring constantly? For many people, the phone is an indispensable convenience and an essential business tool. It can also be a relentless time waster, interrupter and distracter. If your telephone works against you more than for you, here are some ways to turn the tables.

When to use the phone

Use the phone:

- to gain or confirm information more quickly than a visit, memo or e-mail could
- for simple, quick decision-making
- to pass information on quickly
- to set up last-minute appointments or meetings
- for progress reports on important ongoing activities

• to contact a notorious 'talker' or 'socialiser', since it's easier to end a phone conversation than a face-to-face conversation.

> 'The telephone is
> a good way to talk to
> people without having to
> offer them a drink.'
>
> *Frank Lebowitz*

Three situations in which you shouldn't use the phone

• Skip the phone if the information is going to be sent in writing anyway, unless you have a particular reason for 'chatting it through' first.

• If the same message is to go to a number of people, save time by putting it in writing and distributing it (again, unless you have a specific reason for wanting to speak to each person individually).

• If the subject matter is lengthy and complex, it might be better to meet rather than speak on the phone to ensure understanding.

Organise outgoing calls

• Group your calls. Try to do several in one block of time.

• Have the numbers at hand with a note of the points you want to cover to jog your memory: what do you want to say and what do you want to find out? This will save time for both parties and make for more clear, concise communication.

- Have any files or other information you will need ready to hand.
- Respect the other person's time by asking: 'Are you free to talk for a few minutes?'

Control incoming calls

- Consider ways to give yourself some blocks of phone-free time when you can concentrate fully on Value-adding matters. Depending on your job, this could be daily or weekly.
- Route incoming calls to someone else who could field your calls or take messages for an agreed period, say one or two hours. Return the favour and work on filing, Marginal tasks and other low-concentration jobs when you are on 'phone duty'.
- Stand occasionally when you answer the telephone. This will boost your circulation and reduce your fatigue from sitting too long.
- Could someone screen your calls for a while?
- If a known 'talker' phones, say you're in the middle of something and ask if you can ring back. Return the call about 15 minutes before the end of the day or before a meeting you know the person has to attend.
- Consider using your voice mail when you need to concentrate. Accumulate several messages, assemble any information you need to handle the calls, and return them in batches throughout the day.
- When you use your voice mail, resist the temptation to check a message each time one comes in!
- Avoid overusing or constantly using your voice mail. When you use it, request that callers leave a message of who they are, how and when would be best for you to contact them, and what they need to speak to you about. Say when you will be available if they would prefer to phone you back.
- If someone has caught you at a bad time, don't feel trapped to talk right then. Explain it isn't a good time for you right now and agree a time when it will be convenient for you both to talk. Also agree who will phone whom.

End calls cordially

- End calls with talkative people gently: 'OK, thanks for calling. I'd better let you get back to work now.'
- Before ringing off, summarise any action that has been agreed or conclusions arrived at.

Respect other people's time

- Don't use your voice mail to screen calls for hours on end. This wastes the time of other people who need to speak with you.
- Try standing up when you talk on the phone. Your voice will take on a more 'urgent' tone, which will encourage people to be more business-like and 'to the point'.
- Return calls to avoid seeming rude, unreliable and disorganised.

Avoid phone tag

- Try using e-mail or fax to get your message through.
- Leave a message explaining why and by when you need to speak to the person and how and when they can best contact you (including e-mail and fax contact).
- Try to find out a good time for you to call back.
- It has been said that the best time to make and return phone calls is the first two hours of the morning and the last two hours of the afternoon. This is when people are more likely to be available.

Handle visitors harmoniously

Are you plagued by drop-in 'visitors' who interrupt your flow of thought and flow of work? If so, here are some tips to try out:

- If someone is seeking information, are you the best person to supply it? If not, steer them in the right direction.
- When advice is being offered, do you need it? Would it be more

'People try to divert me by
sending lots of stuff into my in-tray,
but I actually plan my work so I've got time to
focus on the things that are important to me, and
I program that into my diary . . . Lots of defence
industry people and others want to see me. The
general rule is I'll see them but they get a strict
15 minutes . . . and then they're out. You've just
got to be ruthless in how you use your time.
I am, because time is the only thing you
haven't got enough of.'

Defence Department Secretary Dr Allan Hawke,
quoted in the Australian Financial Review's
magazine, Boss, June 2000.

helpful in writing? ('Would you mind sending me a memo on
that so I'll be able to refer to it? . . . to think it over when I have
more time?')

- With work-related visits, is this the best timing for you? If not,
could you make another more mutually convenient time to
meet?

- Should someone else be present to prevent you having to repeat
the same discussion points to them?

- Have a mental (or written) list of 'important' phone calls you
need to make and make one. ('Sorry, it's important I ring this
person now.')

- If you don't need to give your undivided attention to the
discussion, ask if your visitor would mind if you did some filing
or other such chores while you talk. (This will also show your
time is valuable.)

- Keep looking at your watch.
- Stand up to talk.
- If all else fails: 'Sorry, I'd love to talk and I'd like to catch up with you later. I really must be getting on now; I have a lot to do.'

Tips for team leaders

Do you respect your team's time? Here is a quick checklist.

- Hold off communicating routine matters until an appropriate time when the team or team members can give you their full attention.
- Set aside regular times to meet with employees. Save queries for those periods.
- Be even-handed with your time for team members.
- Conduct short and to-the-point team meetings to discuss matters of common interest.

In offices

- Don't sit facing the door or corridor. People can catch your attention more easily and interrupt you.
- Lunch together with colleagues. This allows for social contact that might otherwise result in a visit.

Visits by peers

- Don't have a chair by your desk.
- Keep a pen in hand, poised for action.
- Mention the priorities you are working on.

Visits by your manager

- Accommodate your manager. His or her time is valuable, too.
- If the visit is social, and you're really busy, gently switch topics to your progress on the task you are currently working on.

Share offices agreeably

People around us can energise or distract us. Here are some tips for setting out and organising shared office space.

- Group people with common work interests in the same area.
- Traffic ways should not cut through any group or department.
- Place people who frequently come and go or move around a lot near natural traffic areas.
- When seated, no-one should be able to overlook another person's work.
- Put partitions around work areas. Use filing cabinets as room dividers and plants to absorb noise (and give out oxygen for energy).
- Turn the 'ringing tone' on the phones down to avoid jarring people's concentration.
- Arrange your work area so that things you need are conveniently close at hand.
- If important items that you always need 'mysteriously disappear', keep them in a secret place that only you know about. Having to search for basic essentials is frustrating.
- Hold meetings or work-related conversations in smaller adjoining rooms to avoid disturbing others.
- Use computer terminals for electronic communication (but don't 'overuse' this technology).

'You know how you hate to be interrupted, so why are you always doing it to me?'

Author unknown

CHAPTER 12

Work smarter

How to get on with Value-adding activities

Even if you find it hard to concentrate at times during the day, or you find yourself waiting around for someone or something, you can make the most of your time.

Defeat diversions and slow starts to the day

Richard Whately, the former Archbishop of Dublin, once said:

'Lose an hour in the morning and you will spend
all day looking for it.'

If you're not a 'morning person' and you peak later in the day, it's still important to get off to a good start. You can accomplish worthwhile things right from the outset, even if it's only mundane system-imposed activities or other non-productive but necessary work.

Don't waste time waiting for your prime time.

- Don't start your day planning. The press of other activities can all too easily distract you and prevent you from completing your plans. Also, only the urgent matters, not the Value-adding ones, may find their way onto your list.
- Try updating your To Do list before you go home. Or develop next week's plan at the end of each week.
- Set daily priorities based on your Key Result Areas. Highlight the 'musts' (top priorities) or use the ABC system (see Chapter 9). Start with the most important task for the day and work your way down to the least important. Don't start with the small Marginal jobs and work your way up—you may not get there!
- Review your priorities during the day to determine whether any adjustments are necessary.
- Don't start the day working through your in-tray or checking your e-mails just because 'they're there'. Get straight onto important tasks so you will have accomplished something early on.

- Know what your first productive activity will be. It may pay to do some brief preparatory work for that first task so you have made a 'psychological' start.
- What time of day are you most productive? Work on difficult or critical tasks then.
- Don't waste time on the Web. Before you know it, hours can pass. Set yourself a time target each time you log on.
- Don't open e-mail from people you don't know or with subject lines that are irrelevant to you. Trash them straight away.
- Unsubscribe from any newsletters you don't really need.
- Can't bear to miss out? If something is interesting but not essential (print it out if it's electronic) pop it into a To Read file to browse through in your down time. Date each document you add and if any have been there for more than two months dump them! You've lived without reading them this long, so you'll survive. If you think you won't, schedule time to read it in the next week.

Take advantage of your down time

What do you do when you're waiting to see someone, standing in a queue, waiting for or sitting on a bus or a plane, or have a few minutes to kill waiting for the kettle to boil? One thing you can't recycle is wasted time, so here are some ideas to banish lost time.

- Make a list of people you can telephone while you're waiting. Jot down their phone numbers and dot points of what you want to discuss to jog your memory.
- If you're meeting at someone else's office for the first time, ask where the best place to park is. They may have a visitor's car park you can use. Ask about the best route to take, if you're not sure.
- Use your down time to read, think, make notes, or simply relax.
- Always carry with you something to read and a note pad.
- Do some isometric exercises!
- Breathe deeply to exercise your lungs and oxygenate your brain.

- Practise your posture or pelvic floor exercises.
- Keep your brain ticking over by carefully observing your surroundings and seeing how many details you can notice.
- Carry portable tasks to do, articles to read, etc for when you're waiting or travelling.

CHAPTER 13

Pacify paperwork

Overpower paper!

'We can lick gravity, but sometimes the paperwork is overwhelming.'

Wernher von Braun, 1912–1977
Rocket engineer

Dealing with information, whether in electronic or paper form, can take up an enormous amount of time. Save it or toss it? Where do we save it? How do we label it? How do we find it again when we need it?

Being efficient is more about the small things—such as arranging the way we store and retrieve information—than the big things.

Some general tips

- If your system is electronic, make sure you make frequent back-ups.

- If your system is paper-based, store current or active files close to where you sit. Many desks have drawers that will accommodate the files you use most regularly. Store less used files further away.

- The same holds true for discs of documents. You don't need to store them all right next to your computer. Save that space for the few you work with constantly. Put the rest well away.

- Don't start the day on e-mails, especially if this is a productive time of day for you. Instead, begin on an 'A', Value-adding task and allocate a block of time to it, instead of wasting your time on e-mails.

- Check your e-mails when you have a low energy period, when you want a quick break, or at the end of the day (fewer people will respond immediately).

- Deal with each e-mail as you read it as follows: act on anything that will take less than two minutes. Transfer more complex things to an action file. Discard everything else.

- Help others out by keeping your responses short (but not abrupt or curt). Limit the lines in your first and last paragraphs to three. Keep to five lines for main paragraphs.

- If people are sending you information you don't need, let them know. Suggest who in your team would be a better recipient.

- If they're asking you for information that someone else is better equipped to provide, let them know this, too.

- Sort through your in-tray and e-mail two or three times a day (only). (Don't worry: anything truly urgent is likely to arrive in person or via the telephone.)

- Avoid the temptation to check each time something is dropped in your in-tray or your computer chirps that e-mail has arrived: this is a huge time waster. (Keep your in-tray away from your desk and your e-mail disconnected if the temptation is too great!) This way, you'll deal with incoming work when it suits you and stay on top of your To Do list. Face it: your in-tray will never be empty and there will always be waiting e-mails!

- Are you part of a team that communicates electronically? Agree a set of code subject titles to indicate the nature and importance of messages you send each other. This will help you decide whether to read them now or save them for later.

- Don't assume you need a hard copy of every e-mail. Printing things out you really don't need wastes time and paper.

Drowning in documents? Hold a clean-up day

- If you have thousands of e-mails sitting on your system, select a cut-off date and delete everything before that date. If you can't bear to do that, create an 'archive' file and stick them in there. You'll probably never use it, but do it if it will make you feel more comfortable!

- Do the same with unfiled papers. Select a cut-off date and toss everything before that date away. Again, if you can't bear to do that, empty a filing cabinet drawer of hanging files and drop them in there. Pop a coloured piece of paper with the date on it on the top, so you know that everything beneath that paper is older.

- If papers continue to pile up, keep piling them into that filing cabinet drawer. Separate each month with a coloured piece of paper and date it. Should you need to retrieve something, this will make it easier to locate.
- Never allow piles of paper to build up. Ruthlessly file or dump them.
- Be ruthless with your digital documents, too. Keep culling.
- After you've deleted or thrown out unnecessary documents, organise the rest into a useful filing system.

Set up a fabulous filing system

'I write down everything I want to remember. That way, instead of spending a lot of time trying to remember what it is I wrote down, I spend time looking for the paper I wrote it on.'

Beryl Pfizer

It sounds like Beryl needs a fabulous filing system. If you do too, you'll find some help below.

- Label files clearly and meaningfully so you won't waste time searching for them.
- If your files are electronic, take the extra few seconds to set up meaningful folders and subcategories. Make sure they reflect the needs of your business and personal life.
- Make sure your (electronic) file and directory names are long enough to show specifically the contents of the file.
- Make effective use of subfiles, too, whether paper-based or electronic. For example, don't throw everything to do with communication, management, marketing, etc into one big file. Instead, make subcategories of each one.

- If you use paper-based files, make sure you have all the accoutrements you'll need: hanging files, manila files, file tabs and labels. That way, you'll have no excuses for not creating new files the minute you need them.
- Organise your hanging files alphabetically by category.
- Clearly label both the hanging file and the tab of the manila file. Use a thick marker to label the latter.
- If you use paper and electronic systems in parallel, make sure they mirror each other in their pathing and terminology.

Are you a hoarder or a thrower? If you're a hoarder, you may need to learn that not everything is worth keeping. Here are some tips for deciding whether to hoard or throw incoming paperwork.
Ask yourself:

- Will it help me make a decision? (If no, dump it.)
- Is saving it worth the cost and hassle of storing it? (If no, dump it.)
- If I had to pay for this document, would I buy it? (If no, dump it.)
- If I needed this information, could I obtain it from someone else? (If yes, dump it.)
- Have I used this type of information in the past? (If no, dump it.)
- Am I likely to use this information in the future? (If no, dump it.)
- Is an electronic copy readily available? (If yes, dump it.)

Keep your filing system working for you

- Use the 4 Ds to deal with incoming documents only once. When you read a memo, fax, or e-mail, for example, take appropriate action straight away:

1 Deal with it now or at least add some value to it by doing something to progress it before you move on.

2 Delay it by filing it away for future reference, scheduling when you will attend to it, or adding it to your To Do list.

3 Delegate it to someone who is better able to deal with it than you.

4 Dump it.

- Once you've read incoming e-mails and deleted those you don't need, file any you need to keep in designated mailboxes. Label them clearly for easy retrieval.

- Avoid filing everything. Research by Stanford University shows that we never look a second time at 87 per cent of the documents we file. So screen documents ruthlessly. You can probably throw away or delete a lot more than you think.

- Date the documents you do keep. This means all of them: those that you receive, create, and even notes you take.

- When a social or business invitation arrives, decide whether you have the time to go and want to go. If yes, RSVP now, diarise the function, and toss or file the invitation.

- Regularly delete unwanted e-mails, including your folders and sent mail. Make this a routine task whenever you want to take a mental break.

- Every time you create a new document, place it in the correct directory straight away. If you don't do it now, going back to do it will become a task in itself and you probably won't bother. This will start you down the slippery slope to debilitating documentary disorganisation.

- If your paperwork begins piling up (electronically or physically), take the time to clear it up. You're unlikely to have more time to do this tomorrow or the next day, so do it now before it becomes too time-consuming and you have to hold another clean-up day!

- Purge your files periodically. Discard any you clearly will not need. Separate any inactive files from the active files.

Avoid post-holiday horrors

- Ask someone to check and sort through your e-mail, voice mail and in-tray while you are away. They can deal with important items, and organise the rest in order of priority for you.

- When you come back, block out the first day to catch up with your manager, colleagues and work team and to go through and deal with your in-tray and e-mails. Plan and prioritise how you will use the rest of the week to best effect. Don't start anything new, just play 'catch up'.

Information overload?

It's important to keep up-to-date. In fact, if your qualifications are over five years old and you haven't read any current books in your field and aren't keeping up-to-date with relevant journals, you're probably out-of-date!

The trouble is, the amount of information available to us is enormous and growing every day. For example, in the field of business management, over 50,000 new publications are produced every year around the world.

We all need to stay current but if we read everything available, we'd have time for little else. So what can you do? Here are some ideas.

- Assess each journal and periodical you currently receive. How much do you really gain from each? If it's only the occasional worthwhile article, drop your subscription. Read only those that consistently provide valuable information, say at least two good articles per issue.
- Link forces with others. Form a group of people interested in the same topics, for example, in your office or professional organisation. Divide up wading through the mass of information (the books and journals in your interest area(s)). Draw people's attention to those of real interest. Many eyes make lighter work.
- Introduce mini-workshops at work. Every month, people can take turns presenting a ten- to 30-minute summary of latest trends based on reading, a seminar they've attended, or their own work. This takes preparation on the part of this month's presenter, but several people learn quickly and the workload is shared around.
- Attend workshops and seminars presented by experts in the field.

If the speakers offer high quality content, this is a good quick way of absorbing new thinking, new procedures, and new ideas. If you're disappointed, make sure you let the organisers know.

- Don't ignore the importance of reading for pleasure. It gives your brain a rest and increases your thinking power and creativity.
- Always have something with you to read. Even if you catch only a few minutes here and there, you're learning something and spending your time more wisely than letting your eyes and thoughts glaze over!

CHAPTER **14**

Stop spreading yourself too thin!

How not to do a million things at once

DID YOU DELEGATE TO THE RIGHT PERSON?

There is never enough time ... unless you are serving it.

Are you so busy doing so many things for so many people your life feels like a prison sentence at times? Do you sometimes feel pushed and pulled in all directions? Are there never enough hours in the day? Do you have so much on the go that you never seem to complete anything? Are you always rushing around but not accomplishing anything?

First check how swamped you really are. List all the things you need to do, then analyse them. Do a quick reality check to make sure that neither your job nor one of your own personal goals is placing unreasonable demands on you. If the latter is the case, lighten up!

If you are over-extended in your job, ask your boss for advice on how to squeeze it all in. Discuss your Key Result Areas, clarify your goals, and agree your priorities. If your workload really is too high, can you adjust it by changing the parameters of a project, extending a deadline, or narrowing a project's focus, for example?

Perhaps you are overwhelmed with a long list of tasks? Are a lot of them monkeys that someone else should be doing? How many are you procrastinating over? How many are you actually working on? What's stopping you making progress on the others? Are there any patterns in the tasks you are not making progress on; for example, all large projects, team projects, mundane tasks? Have you made a start but lost focus?

Plan a way to complete any tasks like this over the next few weeks. You might divide them into 'bite-sized pieces', work on them for 20 minutes every day, or delegate some of the subtasks that you don't have time for.

If you still believe you are spread too thin, read on.

Some general tips

- Learn how to say 'No'—nicely. Make it a general rule to accept only work that will add value to your job or your life. If you decide to make an exception, do so for a good reason: to strengthen relationships, to help the department or organisation as a whole achieve an objective, to help out a customer, and so on.

- Focus! Review your priorities and keep them in mind as you choose what to do now, what to do later and what not to do at all.

- Use the **RAPT** formula to plan your week. What *R*esults do you want to see by the end of it? Write these as goals and prioritise them. What *A*ctivities do you need to complete to achieve them? List and sequence them. What *P*eriod of time will each activity take? *T*imetable when you will do each activity so you won't overlook any. You'll be rapt with how well this works!

- If you're like most people, you probably can't do everything. Accept that. Set priorities for the day and concentrate on these. If necessary, review and reset priorities each hour! Do the most important things first.

- Some small tasks may not need to be completed to perfection and some do not need to be completed at all. Learn to recognise tasks you are *over-completing*; that is, spending too much time on. It is possible to spend too much time for too few results.

- Avoid taking work home unless you are sure you will do it; opt to stay until the work is finished so you can enjoy your free time.

- When new work comes in, assess how much value it will add and whether it needs to be done right now or whether it can wait until a more convenient time. Think through the 4 Ds: Should I deal with it now? Should I delegate it? Should I delay it until a better time? Should I dump it? If you decide to delay it, add it to your To Do list. If you decide to delegate it, add it to your To Do list or Meet File.

- Each week, decide what your *top three*

'It's not enough to be industrious—so are the ants. What are you industrious about?'

Henry David Thoreau, 1817–1862
US writer

projects will be. These will be three things that add the most value to your life or your job. Focus your thoughts and direct your efforts at completing them. Post them on your desk, on your computer, on your refrigerator, or on your bathroom mirror so they'll be constantly at the front of your mind.

Learn to Delegate

Do you think you are already delegating everything you can? Are you *really*? Think about all your recurring duties and tasks. Think about your projects: could you enlist any help? Think about the things you do that would make an ideal development opportunity for someone. Is anyone already able to do some of these tasks? Would any of these tasks increase an employee's job interest? Are you really delegating all you could?

- Choose the delegate carefully, based on one or more of five criteria:

  1 Who is *interested* in it?

  2 Who can do it now?

  3 Who would like to *learn* it?

  4 Who has the needed skills or attributes?

  5 Who could add it to their *other duties* without becoming overwhelmed with work?

- Don't delegate boring, 'go-fer' work, confidential matters, discipline, or highly 'sensitive' tasks.
- Delegate interesting tasks and projects too, not just routine ones.
- Delegate a task if your're not adding any value.
- Always explain the importance of a delegated task, how it fits

into the bigger picture, and why you've selected this person (for training, to develop skills, etc).

- Clearly outline the result or end product you are looking for and the standards you expect. Explain in terms of *quality*, *quantity*, *safety*, *cost*, *accuracy*, *service levels* and *time*.

- Discuss the resources available to the delegate, the time frame, and what to do if he/she needs help.

- If the task is long or complex, or if the delegate has a tendency to procrastinate, focus on starting the job, not finishing it. Don't say 'And I'd like to have that report a month from now', but 'When do you think you can start writing a rough outline?'

- Check to make sure you have explained clearly.

- Except for people you are training, stress results, not details. In other words, delegate the *what's* and the *results* but not the *how's*.

> Remember US President John F Kennedy? He told NASA 'Get a man on the moon by the end of the decade and bring him back safely to earth.' There were two parts to this: *What* he wanted done and the *results* he expected. That's how to delegate!

- If the delegated task is a development opportunity for the delegate, train the delegate thoroughly.

- Agree clear, quantifiable, concrete objectives.

- Follow up. Delegation is not 'hit and run'. It is not 'dumping' boring tasks either.

- Develop a monitoring plan. You don't want to do the task for the delegate, but by the same token, you have a responsibility to check often enough so that if things are going 'off the rails', you can get them 'back on track'. You want the job done right, after all!

- On longer tasks or projects, agree critical milestones for follow up and when you will meet to follow up.

- Save time with 'management by exception': 'If I don't hear from you beforehand, I'll expect it Wednesday.'
- Don't take back something once you've delegated it.
- Keep your distance when you delegate. Over-managing will take up nearly as much of your time as doing the job yourself! If you think the delegate will need a lot of help, plan plenty of monitoring and coaching sessions, or give the task to someone better equipped to do it.
- To stop looking over a delegate's shoulder, ask yourself: 'Do I need to worry about this any more?' If the answer is 'Yes', arrange for regular updates; if it is 'No', let the delegate get on with the job.
- Give plenty of positive and specific feedback. When people do a good job, say so! If they think you haven't noticed, they'll think you don't care. If they think you don't care, they'll think the job isn't important after all. In that case, why bother to continue doing it well? Make sure people know you appreciate their efforts to keep their performance high.
- Keep a delegation log. When you delegate an assignment, jot it down. This could be, for example, in a special file of your electronic task manager or on a special section of your To Do list.
- It may take some time to explain or train someone to do a recurring task (one that will be done over and over). However, the time you spend explaining and training will be repaid many times over in the future.
- Follow monkey management principles:
  - Help people solve problems they run into but don't solve them for them.
  - Turn their questions around. Ask monkey bearers for suggested solutions. (See also Chapter 4.)
- Take one thing off your To Do list and delegate it. *Right now!*

If work is not up to your standard . . .

Respond calmly to mistakes. See what you can both learn from them.

Discuss it in private.

Be a coach not a critic.

Focus on the work not the person.

Fix the problem, not the blame.

Ask for their suggestions on improvement.

Focus on the future: 'Next time, . . .' 'From now on . . .'

Were you available for consultation?

Delegation plan

Here are five questions to help you select work that is suitable for delegation:

1. Which tasks can I delegate, especially recurring tasks? (Warning: don't delegate boring, mundane tasks, things that are confidential or sensitive, or high cost, high risk, unpleasant or disagreeable jobs.)

2. Who would be suitable to pick up each task?

3. What standards do I require (time, cost, quality, accuracy, quantity, safety, service levels, etc)?

4. What are the constraints?

5. What resources are available to the delegate?

Five levels of monitoring

Select from five levels of monitoring, depending on the employee's level of skills and experience on the one hand and their willingness to do the task on the other.

149

Level 1: Just do it!

This is for people who are competent and willing. You can safely assign them the work and let them get on with it, provided you have warning signals in place that will alert you to any potential problems.

Level 2: Keep me informed

This is for people who are dependable but slightly less skilled, experienced or willing. They can carry on, but should keep you informed of certain key information so that you can satisfy yourself things are progressing well.

Level 3: Check back first

Ask the person to check back with you before proceeding at certain critical points. That way, you can assure yourself that things will be done correctly.

Level 4: Let's talk it through first

Ask the person to decide what to do and to talk it through with you before acting. This is an expanded version of Level 3 and lets you review how the person is thinking and approaching the task. It gives you a chance to coach and develop his/her skills.

Level 5: I'll walk you through it

This is for people new to a task. Train the person carefully and allow time for his/her skills to build.

Seven steps to delegation

If you follow these seven steps to delegation, you'll find you can't go wrong:

1 **Goal:** What end result do I expect?

2 **Reason:** Why is it important? Where does it fit in? Why are you asking *this* person to do it?

3 **Standard:** What standards do I expect?

(4) **Time frame**: What are the expected start and completion times? Are there any time constraints?

(5) **Resources**: What resources (for example, people, funds, equipment) are available to the delegate?

(6) **Help**: Who should the delegate turn to for help or advice? What if you're not available?

(7) **Progress**: How will you and the delegate monitor progress and effectiveness?

When work is delegated to you

Ask enough questions to ensure you know clearly what is expected of you and when it is expected. Ask yourself:

- Do I know how to do this or will I need some training or coaching? Where can I find the information I need?
- Am I clear about the precise end product that is expected (cost, quality, accuracy, time frame, and so on)?
- Do I know what resources I can call on (for example, people and other sources of information, funds, equipment)?
- Am I clear on how my effectiveness will be assessed?
- Do I know how my manager wants me to report progress (for example, how much or how little detail, in writing or verbally, how regularly)?
- How extensive is my authority to make decisions versus referring to my manager for approval?

Acid test: do I understand what I am expected to do well enough to explain it to someone else?

Say 'No' nicely: Avoid monkeys

Did your analysis of your completed Time Logs in Chapter 6 and your identification of your main time wasters in Chapter 8 indicate that you are so busy doing other people's work that you have trouble getting your own done? If so, you need to be more ruthless at planning your days or weeks to highlight and attend to Value-adding, high priority matters, build in some slack time to let you deal comfortably with team members, colleagues and others who may need your help, and learn to say 'No' nicely.

- Don't solve problems for people unless they are incompetent or untrustworthy. If they are incompetent, train them. If they are not trainable or are untrustworthy, why are they working for you? Perhaps it's time to share your doubts and concerns with them candidly and tactfully.
- Don't let monkey bearers off-load their monkey onto your shoulders. When they know what to do, let them know you have every confidence in their ability to get their job done.
- Perhaps they know what to do but want a bit of reassurance. Spend a few minutes chatting through their plan of attack and satisfy yourself they are on the right lines.
- Once you know they're on the right track, tell monkey bearers you'll support them in their efforts to resolve the problem.

BEFORE TELLING MONKEY BEARERS WHAT TO DO, ASK THE FOLLOWING FOUR QUESTIONS:

1. What is the problem? Ask them to explain it in one thorough, objective statement.
2. What are some ways to solve it?
3. What is the best way to solve it?
4. What is the first step to take?

- Learn to say something like: 'I'm really committed now although I could give you some time tomorrow' or 'You sound really busy and I'd love to help but I'm committed to a couple of high priority things just now.'
- Make sure your staff include a 'recommended actions' section in all their reports.

- You can't say 'Yes' to everything. Decide what your priorities are and say 'No' to everything else.
- One way to say 'No' nicely is to explain you have a commitment to do something else. Specify what it is, if you want to. This sounds more official and serious than saying 'I have to do something else' or simply, 'I can't', or 'I haven't got time'.

Reduce boss-imposed time

Is your boss constantly assigning work to you, checking to see how you are getting on, or telling you step by step how to do things? Maybe your boss needs to learn how to delegate. Or maybe you need to build up your boss's trust in you and your ability to manage your time and carry out your work both effectively and efficiently.

- The more 'on top' of your job you are, the less you will experience boss-imposed time.
- Be ready to show your manager your list of goals and your To Do list. Involve her/him in re-assessing priorities if you are becoming overloaded. Your boss probably has a wider view of the organisation's objectives and needs, so make use of that.
- Discuss your Key Result Areas to make sure you both see your job the same way.
- Make sure you have a way to measure all outcomes you're expected to achieve.
- Keep lines of communication open: provide formal and informal progress reports. Ask for formal and informal appraisals.
- Even if you see your boss every day, have a standing arrangement to meet weekly or fortnightly. Have an agenda that covers progress on current projects, anything that is impinging on your ability to achieve your goals, successes and goals achieved, anything you need help with, problems you have resolved or are working on, and generally how things are going.
- Have the 'hard numbers' available, especially if your boss is a

'numbers person'. Present the data in a format that's easy to understand; for example, in tables, graphs or pie charts.

- Work with your manager's priorities. What would make him/her most happy if you achieved them? What is in your boss's 'world'? What issues and concerns are uppermost in your boss's mind? What are your boss's organisational and personal goals? What pressures are on your boss from his/her own boss and colleagues?

- Fit in with your manager's preferred working style. Does your manager prefer to receive information through memos, formal meetings or informal discussions? Does your manager like to know all the details or just the end result? Is he/she task-focused or more people-oriented? Knowing these things will help you fit in with your manager's working style and support him/her better. If you don't know the answers to these questions, you are flying blind and misunderstandings are inevitable.

- See yourself as your boss's partner in achieving results and meeting priorities.

- Report problems early on before they grow. Take the facts with you, together with a proposed way of dealing with or rectifying the problem.

- If your boss delegates something to you, make sure you are completely clear on what is expected of you (goals, time lines, etc), constraints, limits of your authority, resources available and so on.

- If you're not fully trained in the task, make sure your boss is aware of this and is willing to coach you or nominate someone else to coach you through it. You don't want to be micro-managed, which will increase boss-imposed time, so your boss must feel comfortable that you are able to carry out the job or able to get help if you need it.

FIVE QUESTIONS
TO ASK YOUR BOSS

- What are my Key Result Areas and main goals?
- What operating guidelines do you want me to work within?
- How will we measure my performance?
- How do you prefer to receive progress reports and general information?
- How can I help you do your job better?

Maybe you already know the answers to these questions. What does that tell you about your boss and the organisation you work for?

Manage meetings marvellously

Defeat the curse of meaningless meetings

Whether around a table, or through a video conference, teleconference or the Internet, meetings have the potential to waste enormous amounts of time. If some of the meetings you attend run on and achieve little, frustrate participants, and generally waste your time, the following tips will help you make good use of meetings.

> 'Meetings are indispensable when you don't want to do anything.'
>
> *John Kenneth Galbraith, 1908–*
> *US economist*

When to call a meeting

Call a meeting when:

- there is no better or less expensive way to achieve the result (for example, face-to-face, over the telephone, or in writing by memo, fax or e-mail)
- you need other people to help solve problems or implement solutions or decisions
- you need to gather or exchange information and opinions
- you need to generate discussion or ideas
- you need to pass on or explain information personally; for example, when the information to be shared:
  - is complex or controversial
  - has major implications for the meeting members
  - needs to be heard from a particular person
  - there is symbolic value in giving the information personally
  - some discussion or information exchange is required
  - clarification or comments are needed to help people make sense of the information
  - the information needs to be presented quickly and you don't want to write it.

When to skip meetings

Skip meetings when:

- there is nothing specific to discuss
- you've already made up your mind
- you don't need input from others
- involving others would only complicate matters
- the meeting is just a substitute for real work or a stalling device
- the meeting is only to rubber-stamp a decision
- the meeting is a power trip
- there is no agenda.

When someone asks to see you

- Ask what they want to talk to you about and what they hope to achieve from the meeting. You may need to prepare, even if only mentally.
- Find out how long they think the meeting will take, explaining that you want to make sure you set enough time aside.
- Agree on a mutually convenient time to meet.
- If the person needs to see you now and you can't delay it, take a moment to note down what you were doing and the next steps before taking a deep breath and giving the person your full concentration and attention. When you're finished, your note will remind you of what to carry on with.

Gain the agenda advantage

- Any meeting worth holding is worth planning. Devote plenty of time to planning and preparing meetings with specific agendas.
- Write action-based agendas (to decide, to generate options, to develop a draft plan, to review progress and plan next steps, etc).

- Put the important items up front on the agenda if you want to encourage people to arrive on time.
- Include a finish time to help people concentrate.
- Send out the agenda and any background information about a week in advance, stressing the importance of preparation. To keep the meeting flowing, participants will need to be ready to ask and answer questions.
- Try to keep the numbers below 12. Hold two separate meetings if necessary to ensure everyone will be able to contribute fully and to make it easier to hold everyone's attention.
- Follow the two-thirds rule: each person present should be involved in or concerned with two out of every three agenda items. Otherwise, the meeting will waste *their* time!

Chair a meeting with class

- Be there first so you can greet people as they arrive. This sets the scene and establishes a friendly and open atmosphere.
- Make sure people are comfortable, but not too comfortable or the meeting may drag on longer than necessary!
- Start on time, even if everyone hasn't arrived. If you start late, you penalise those who were on time and reward the latecomers.
- Open on a pleasant note by welcoming people and thanking them for attending. Say a few words about what you hope the meeting will achieve.
- Review and confirm the agenda. This makes sure everyone understands the issues and why they are being discussed, and orients them to the content of the meeting. It also signals the importance of the agenda and encourages people not to drift away from it.
- Unless you need to provide information, limit your contributions to one comment or question at a time.
- See your primary role as assisting the participants to achieve the meeting's goals.

- Establish a friendly, supportive climate to encourage contributions and ideas.
- Guide the discussion, don't dominate it.
- Help members build on each other's experience and knowledge.
- Make sure all sides get equal 'air time'.
- Keep the discussion on track by sticking to the agenda. No rambling 'shop talk', red herrings or soap boxes!
- Explore all points of view, especially those that aren't your own. This will help you avoid using 'the power of the chair' to dominate the meeting.
- Use differences of opinion as opportunities to explore issues more deeply.
- Encourage people to provide information and express their ideas.
- Summarise often.
- Clarify any unclear points.
- Don't let people masquerade their opinions as facts.
- Close a discussion when it is clear that:
  - consensus has been reached
  - more facts are needed before further progress can be made
  - meeting members need more time to think or discuss something with colleagues not present
  - events are changing rapidly and are likely to alter the basis of discussion quite soon
  - there is not enough time to discuss the issue fully
  - two or three members can settle the matter outside the meeting without taking up the time of everyone present.
- Record all decisions and agreements and keep a note of all action items.
- When you close a meeting, clarify what will happen next: who is responsible for doing what and by when. Double-check that all decisions and actions to be taken have been recorded and, if appropriate, fix the time and place of the next meeting.
- Thank people for their time and participation and spend a few minutes talking about how well the meeting went and what it accomplished. End on a positive note.
- Follow up action items and decisions.

Video conferences

- Ask participants to use large name cards if they don't know each other.
- Before you begin, introduce everyone if necessary and provide a bit of background information so everyone knows how the other members can potentially contribute.
- Clarify people's roles. Who will operate the camera? What will happen if the connection breaks?
- Never interrupt a speaker.
- Don't shift and move about in your chair or tap pencils, shuffle feet, etc. The microphone will pick it up as distracting background noise.
- Don't lean into the camera, toward listeners; this will look too aggressive. Stay seven to ten feet back from the camera.
- Keep reasonably still and refrain from hand gestures to avoid creating distractions. Use slower and smaller movements than you would in a face-to-face meeting.
- Have a predetermined procedure for asking, acknowledging and dealing with questions.
- Remember, people can see you even if you aren't the one talking. Mind your body language!
- If you need to have a side discussion, use the mute button to avoid the microphone picking it up and the camera re-focusing onto you.

Teleconferences

- Before you begin, clarify people's roles. Who will call the others in case the connection breaks?
- Have a predetermined procedure for asking, acknowledging and dealing with questions.
- In a teleconference you can't see everyone and it's easy to forget who is actually 'present'. Draw your own 'map' to keep fully

tuned in: write the names of those present on a piece of paper and put it in front of you. If it helps, draw it out as you would if people were sitting around a conference table.

- Never interrupt a speaker.
- Don't shift and move about in your chair or tap pencils, shuffle feet, etc. The telephone will pick it up as distracting background noise.
- Don't hold side conversations.
- Keep your attention from wandering by keeping notes of who is saying what.
- If people don't know you well, state your name when you begin speaking.

Participating in meetings

'The only time I am conscious of the time is when I'm on time. Then, I am frankly astonished.'

George Sava

- Prepare thoroughly by thinking through the objectives, working out the issues that will need to be addressed and gathering the information you will need.
- Arrive on time. Tardiness is disrespectful to others.
- Bring any necessary information and paperwork, with copies for others if this would be helpful.

- Stay focused on the goals of the meeting.
- Speak up when you have something to say, keeping your comments brief and to the point.
- Make your comments clear and loud enough to be heard.
- Use up only your share of the speaking time. Organise your thoughts before speaking, either in your head or by jotting down

a few reminder notes. This saves everyone's time and projects a positive impression.

- Omit personal stories unless they make a point, and skip 'inside jokes'.
- When speaking, address the entire meeting (or the chair in a more formal meeting), not just one meeting member.
- Don't play 'devil's advocate' for the sake of it.
- Don't 'dump data'. Have supporting evidence but don't bore people with it or take up precious meeting time with it. If people have questions, pull out some of your detailed information.
- Avoid one-on-one discussions and conversations.
- Keep the floor by saying: 'I have three points I'd like to make on this issue. First, . . .' Number your points as you go and keep them brief.
- Disagree without being disagreeable. Paraphrase (using neutral language) what the other person has said before expressing your reservations, concerns or confusion, in a way that shows you are open to hearing the answer.
- Don't disagree with an idea or proposal unless you have an alternative to offer.
- If you're asked to contribute and you have nothing to add, say so.
- Keep your own special interests in check and don't digress, ramble or sidetrack the discussion.
- Listen to others and respect that their ways might be different to yours.
- Work to resolve conflicts.
- Check out what people mean.

'The surest way to be late
is to have plenty of time.'

Author unknown

Managing minutes magnificently

- Good meeting minutes show the action items each participant is responsible for achieving and the target date. Use them in conjunction with your own notes to make sure you keep to your commitments.
- If you can't do all of the actions for which you are responsible straight away, add them to your To Do list with the target dates.
- Update your copy of the minutes as soon as you've attended to the action items you're responsible for to reflect what you've done.
- If you're using an electronic system, cut and paste your action items from the minutes to your task manager to save time.

CHAPTER 16

Manage projects productively

Time-saving strategies for orderly and successful projects

'The sooner you fall
behind, the more time you
have to catch up.'

Sam Ogden

Sam's slogan isn't a particularly sound one when it comes to practical time management! The more complex and/or important a project, the more important it is you plan it wisely and manage it well.

Some general tips

- Keep a list of projects and tasks your staff are working on. You can also note the date they were assigned and the deadline. Use this list to schedule progress meetings.

- Keep a list of your own projects, too, and add to it as new projects are assigned. This list should be an important source for your To Do list.

- If there are a lot of projects on your list, prioritise them.

- Work off your project list and when a project is completed, cross it off.

- Set up and maintain a separate file for each project. Keep all documents related to that project in the file.

- When you are first assigned a project, write a project summary and attach it to the front inside cover of the project file. Describe the project, its objectives, its scope or limits, and its deadline.

Then list the action steps you anticipate taking. Work your way down the steps.

- Allow enough time to complete the project properly and to avoid last-minute panics. Add in an extra margin of time to accommodate setbacks and unforeseen problems.

- If the project is a large one, break it down into stages (or milestones) with target dates. Completing these will give you a sense of accomplishment and progress and keep your motivation high.

- For very important or complex projects, give each one its own To Do list. Break it up into steps, each with a targeted beginning and finish date. List everything you need to do and cross it off as you go along. Update the list as you move through the project. If that's overkill, just list the action steps you need to take for each milestone.

- Involve your staff in planning the projects they will be involved in. This will improve their understanding of the project and their commitment and quality of work.

- If you're not working on the project daily, write notes to yourself on what you've done and what you want to do next. If appropriate, keep a 'things to follow up' list, too.

- Schedule uninterrupted blocks of time to work on important projects. Work on these when you are most alert.

- Meet your deadlines.

- When you finish a project, sort through its file and discard any duplicate and useless documents, then file in your inactive files for future reference.

- Once the project is complete, ask yourself (or the team you have been working with): 'What have I (or we) learned from this that I (or we) can apply to my (our) next project?' Make a note of lessons learned, especially if that type of project is likely to recur. This will provide a learning and continuous improvement focus.

CHAPTER 17

The time is now

How to build new habits

Discipline eventually becomes desire. We eventually look forward to doing something and eventually, doing it becomes a part of us. We can do it no other way.

BETTER WAYS

Craig's crusade against clutter

Craig was fed up with wasting time searching for things. He began a concerted effort to keep his work area clear of everything but what he was actually working on. He spent the best part of an afternoon finding 'homes' for things and giving his workspace a thorough clean. He loved the look of it!

For the first week or so, it was easy to keep putting things away when he finished using them—he just kept reminding himself to do it. Then it became automatic. After several months, he noticed that his old bad habits had begun to creep back and his work area was becoming messy again. So he renewed his all-out campaign against clutter. This cycle of 'back-sliding' continued for several years, at longer and longer intervals. Each time, Craig renewed his crusade until, finally, tidiness became a permanent habit.

Wendy's wake-up walk

Wendy had never been one for exercise and when she developed her vision for a balanced life, she realised her own health was a sorely neglected facet. She resolved to get up at 6 am every day and join her neighbour walking her dog.

For the first month, she dragged herself out of bed. Slowly, she began to look forward to her morning walks and now, 18 months later, they are such an enjoyable part of her life she would never dream of skipping that 6 am 'wake-up walk'.

Purpose

Your purpose, which we looked at in Chapters 2 and 5, shows you how to manage your time effectively. Make it a habit to focus your time, attention and efforts on things that add value to your life and the contribution you make in your job.

Practice

From reading Chapters 8 through 16, you also know how to 'work smart' and use your time efficiently. It's now up to you to build the habits that help you achieve more in a day.

Process

In the preceding eight chapters, you have highlighted or circled a myriad of Make Time tips to try out. To simplify things, add structure, and enlist the help of your subconscious brain (more about this in Part 4), look back through them and transfer the most promising ideas to this page.

_____

_____

_____

_____

_____

_____

_____

_____

_____

_____

_____

_____

What will you do first? Which will have the biggest pay-off in terms of Making Time? Which will help you break bad time management habits?

Now select three ideas and commit yourself to applying them consistently for at least three weeks. When the three weeks are up, decide how well each works for you and whether you will keep doing it, adapt it, or dump it.

Once these habits have become part of your normal way of operating, return to this page and select another three ideas to apply consistently for another three weeks. In this way, you will be continually making better use of your time for months to come.

> 'The way to get started is to quit talking and begin doing.'
>
> *Walt Disney, 1901–1966*
> *US film and theme park*
> *entrepreneur*

> 'We are what we repeatedly do. Excellence, then, is not an act, but a habit.'
>
> *Aristotle, 384–322 BC*
> *Greek philosopher*

Banish *'I can't because . . .'*

Do you think you can't get on top of your paperwork, control interruptions, or stop procrastinating? Are you thinking of a million reasons you'll never get better organised or get those monkeys off your back? As long as the reasons *why not* outnumber the reasons *why*, you never will.

As soon as you can think of more reasons why you will and you can, you will! Make sure your positive thoughts outweigh your negative thoughts. Every successful person, in any walk of life, operates this way.

Focus on the reasons you *can* succeed, not the reasons you will fail. This might be difficult at first, but keep at it. In Chapter 19 you will discover how this programs your powerful subconscious to make success certain.

Build lasting habits to make time

'Bad habits are
like a comfortable bed.
Easy to get into but hard
to get out of.'

Author unknown

Sometimes, we're our own worst enemy, especially when it comes to starting fresh routines. Here's how to build Make Time habits that will last:

1. Begin an intense campaign against your old habit.

2. Do not tolerate exceptions until your new habit is firmly established.

3. Begin changing your behaviour as soon as you resolve to change.

Be consistent and persistent

W Somerset Maugham, the English novelist and dramatist, said:

'An unfortunate thing about the world is that good habits are much easier to give up than bad ones.'

That's why we need to put in consistent daily effort to achieve the results we're after.

Do your best every day and don't settle for second best. Susie O'Neill's mental and physical consistency—every day—won her a gold and a silver medal at the Sydney 2000 Olympics.

Your daily habits are the key to your success.

Because overwriting old habits with new ones isn't easy, building new habits often feels like taking three steps forward and one or two back. So make sure you're your own best friend when it comes to building terrific time management habits. Knowing that changing habits is not easy, commit to making the changes you need to make in order to manage your time better. Be persistent.

Every little bit helps. Every little quit hurts.

In the words of Calvin Coolidge, 30th President of the United States:

> *'Nothing in the world can take the place of persistence. Talent will not; nothing is more common than unsuccessful men with talent. Genius will not; unrewarded genius is almost a proverb. Education will not; the world is full of educated derelicts. Persistence and determination alone are omnipotent.'*

Overcome opposition

If change were easy, the planet wouldn't be going through its current turmoil. We'd all be able to change long-standing habits overnight, effortlessly and quickly. We'd all welcome change, in others, and in ourselves, with open arms.

Change may be the norm in nature, but it seems people are conditioned to fret over it, and often: resist it.

There are two types of opposition that concern us when we're trying to build new habits: intrapersonal and interpersonal. The first is resistance from within ourselves and the second is opposition from others.

Internal opposition

'The only reason [habits] persist is that they are offering some satisfaction. You allow them to persist by not seeking any other, better form of satisfying the same needs. Every habit, good or bad, is acquired and learned in the same way—by finding that is a means of satisfaction.'

Juliene Berk

Our habits serve, or once served, some purpose for us. At some level, even our bad time management habits work for us. This is why, through our own time management practices, we may be unwittingly exacerbating some of our time management problems.

This is not to say that all our time management problems are our own fault! Some are a natural part of life and work. We need to find ways to manage better those we can't avoid.

Not all time management problems are unavoidable, though. Perhaps as you read through Part 3 you realised that some of your own time management habits are a contributing factor. Perhaps some of your time management problems are even of your own making!

Whenever we try to build a new habit, we usually need to break an existing one—one that has or had some value for us. This involves re-programming our subconscious. (Although this is not an easy task, it's not as difficult as it sounds either, as you'll see in Chapter 19.) This is why it's so important to be consistent and persistent when building new habits.

Opposition from others

Have you ever tried to 'turn over a new leaf' only to find those around you were hostile to your best intentions? So hostile, in fact, that they tried to sabotage your efforts and 'put you back in your box'? There's a good reason this happens.

In living and working with others, we get to know how people do things. They get to know how we work, too. Together, we find a comfortable balance in the way we operate.

When people change their behaviour, it often alters this balance. This means that if we change a long-standing habit, others may try to thwart it, especially if they don't understand the reasons for the changes. People will resist all the more if they have to make some changes themselves in order to accommodate our change of habit.

The bigger the changes we make, the more uncomfortable others are likely to become. This is the reason people often combat our good intentions to change our habits and try to influence us to go back to our old, predictable and expected routines.

There are three things you can do to turn this around.

1. If appropriate, tell people what you are doing, and why, and how they will benefit. This will often lessen their resistance and spur them to help you in your efforts.

2. As much as you can, avoid making it necessary for them to make any adjustments in order to accommodate the changes you are making.

3. Make your change gradual and non-threatening to others.

Go for small, certain changes

Internal and external opposition can make it difficult to build new habits that last. Not only do we have our older, and usually more

'Little strokes fell great oaks.'

Benjamin Franklin, 1706–1790
US inventor, scientist,
philosopher and statesman

comfortable, 'set ways' and routines beckoning us, others around us are trying to pull us back into the familiar relationships and ways of doing things.

This is why it's often a good idea to introduce new habits gradually, especially if they're going to affect others. This is also why it's a good idea not to make too many big changes at once.

As the saying goes.

'Mile by mile it's a trial. Inch by inch it's a cinch.'

Perceptual lag

Have you ever had the experience of improving the way you do something and others continue to treat you as if you had made no improvement? This is called perceptual lag. Even after we've made a change to the way we do things, people continue to see 'the old us', the image they have built up of us.

'We are all captives of the pictures in our head—our belief that the world we have experienced is the world that really exists.'

Walter Lippmann, 1889–1974
US journalist and author

People see what they expect to see. It may take them a while to adjust, just as it takes us time to build new habits.

Don't let people's perceptual lag discourage you. Keep up the good work regardless! Eventually, others will catch up!

'Persistence makes
the impossible possible,
the possible likely, and the
likely definite.'

Author unknown

PART 4

The final touches

'Until you value yourself, you will not value your time. Until you value your time, you will not do anything with it.'

M. Scott Peck, 1936–
Psychiatrist and author

Mindsets of terrific time managers

CHAPTER 18

What the latest research tells us about making time

CHICKEN LITTLE POULTRY

Why do some people get so much done while others struggle just to get by? The latest psychological research into personal productivity and time management shows that the ways in which we *think* and *live* are more important than the number of hours we invest in a given task.

Any pilot will tell you that the approach to landing a plane is all-important. So is our approach to the way we use our time. Paying attention to the mindsets with which we set about our daily activities can pay big dividends in how much we accomplish.

Manage your mindsets

Our beliefs, views and opinions—about others and ourselves, about time and how to manage it, about how we 'should' and 'should not' do things—become entrenched in our subconscious.

Mindsets direct our behaviour. They set apart the 'best' from the 'good'. Here are eight mindsets that will help you get your mental approach right and manage your time better. The more you adopt them, the more automatic and effortless Making Time will become for you.

> 'Man is made by his beliefs. As he believes, so he is.'
>
> *Bhagavad Gita*
> *Hindu scripture*

Push your personal envelope and love what you do

In your job, do you consciously seek ways to challenge yourself and stretch your skills? Do you get enjoyment from your job? From your personal life?

If you're a terrific time manager, you probably answered 'Yes' to these questions. Why? Because you work more on your 'cutting edge' and find ways to extend yourself and enjoy what you're doing. This increases your productivity and willingness to manage your time effectively.

Psychologists Mihaly Czikszentmihalyi of the University of Chicago and Dean Simonton of the University of California have found that people who find a balance between their skills and the challenges they face are more likely to be productive in whatever they're doing. High achievers spend more time than low achievers 'pushing their own envelopes' and testing and expanding their skills.

Whether you're working or gardening, invent ways to challenge yourself and enjoy what you are doing. This will help you to spend more time being productive.

Do you do things because you *want* to or because you *have* to?

What sort of a job do you do when you *have* to do something? 'Ugh, I *have to* do the dishes', 'I *have to* finish this report.' Most people agree that approaching something from a *have to* point of view results in an unwilling attitude, lack of satisfaction, and a mediocre outcome.

Learn to say 'I want to get these dishes done so the kitchen looks good', or 'I want to finish this report so it's out of the way and I can get on with other work.' (If you can't think of a good and worthwhile reason to do it, are you really sure you need to do it?!)

Great and positive expectations breed success

If you have a setback, do you blame yourself and let it ruin the rest of your day? Or do you take it 'on the chin' and figure it's only temporary? Do you expect the best of yourself, for yourself, and from everyone around you?

> By asking for the impossible, we obtain the best possible.
>
> *Italian proverb*

'Set high standards and expect the best' is a good motto to adopt. Be positive in your expectations so they'll inspire you to achieve your goals.

Some people set high standards, but in a negative, disheartening way. Even after they've achieved their goal, they find something to be gloomy about: 'I could have done/should have done better . . . ' They manage to find something wrong, even the smallest thing. Instead of congratulating themselves, they condemn themselves. This is silly.

If you're a critical high standard setter, stop constantly finding fault with yourself. This drains your energy, confidence and motivation. Congratulations and good feelings are essential to success. They encourage us to keep going until we reach our goal and give us the motivation to do even better next time.

The ancient Greek philosopher Epictetus said:

'Our life is what our thoughts make it.'

Expect great and good things.

Are you an optimist or a pessimist?

If you're a terrific time manager, you're probably also an optimist. You see a glass as half full not half empty and you know that you can fill it right to the top if you want to. This helps you see setbacks as only temporary and expect the best for yourself and from yourself.

Psychologist Martin Seligman says optimism breeds confidence, faith in our abilities, and persistence. This keeps us going when we hit difficult periods and stumble over hurdles. Optimists know that one bad day doesn't mean they're a loser. They can see setbacks as challenges and obstacles as stepping-stones.

If you're a pessimist, learn to be an optimist (or at least be a realist and acknowledge that perhaps the glass is twice as big as it needs to be). Know that one bad day doesn't mean much. Here's how:

• Avoid blaming yourself for your failures.

- Recognise that mistakes usually have only a temporary effect.
- Don't let mishaps or down days in one facet of your life influence other facets of your life.
- Pat yourself on the back whenever you succeed at something or achieve a goal. Think of them as lasting achievements that will pay off.

This has important implications in time management, too. We know from Parkinson's Law (see Chapter 7) that work expands to fill the time available. Research confirms this.

> *The way to get a lot of things done is to expect to*
> *get a lot of things done.*

This way, we are more likely to manage our time so that we actually succeed.

Set high time management standards for yourself and expect to achieve them. As the saying goes:

> *Mediocrity is a choice. So is excellence.*

Choose excellence and work consistently towards it.

THE POWER OF BELIEFS

Richard Lazarus of the University of California at Berkeley found that patients who repressed pre-operation thoughts about the seriousness of their condition and what could go wrong during surgery suffered fewer post-operative complications than patients who dwelt on the dangers of surgery.

Martin Seligman of the University of Pennsylvania found that five years after mastectomy, 75 per cent of women who denied their illness were still alive and healthy versus 35 per cent who had resigned themselves to their fate.

Believing something is so is the first step to making it so.

Do you have faith in yourself that you can be a better time manager?

Unless you believe you have what it takes, you will never manage your time better. Henry Ford, founder of the Ford Motor Company, said:

> *'Whether you believe you can or whether you believe you can't, you're right.'*

We can't make any progress without confidence in our own ability.

WHAT LIMITS DO YOU SET FOR YOURSELF IN YOUR MIND?

Russian Olympian Vasili Alexeev was trying to break a weight-lifting record of 500 pounds. He had lifted 499 many times, but could never make 500. His trainers believed he could do it and decided to 'trick' him. They put 501.5 pounds on the bar and rigged it to look like 499 pounds. Vasili lifted it easily. He knew it was possible! Once he'd lifted 501.5 pounds, other weight-lifters went on to break his record: they, too, knew it was possible.

If you set your sights high, you'll fly!

Be mindful, not mindless and stay focused

Do you ever feel in a rut with your job; that it's just the same old thing, day after day?

'We've always done it this way' thinking leads us to give up and never improve. Psychologist Ellen Langer of Harvard University points out that rigid, automatic thinking leads to what she calls mindlessness. We just go through the motions.

Mindfulness is seeing the novel in the unfamiliar, a kind of flexible and creative style that turns stumbling blocks to building blocks.

Terrific time managers don't get into ruts. They are mindful people who stay focused on their goals. They keep their thoughts, words, deeds and mental pictures sharply focused on what they intend to achieve.

This helps them find solutions to almost anything. They focus not on obstacles but on how to overcome them to reach their goal. They constantly examine what they're doing to find ways to do it better, differently, more efficiently, more easily, more quickly. How can I streamline this? How can I add more value?

This is the *kaizen* mindset of continuous improvement.

> 'Most people spend more time and energy trying to go around problems than trying to solve them.'
>
> *Henry Ford, 1863–1947*
> *Founder of the*
> *Ford Motor Company*

Mindfulness also prevents 'burnout' by motivating people to find innovative solutions, not just to new problems but also to the 'same old problems'. Mindless people burn out when they see the same old problems without solutions. If you're mindful, you know there are multiple solutions to almost anything.

Exercise for energy

In the mornings, do you wake up tired or full of energy? Do you exercise regularly?

If you feel energetic, you'll have a go at tasks you might otherwise leave. A sense of well-being can bolster productivity. It isn't completed tasks that make us tired, but worrying about tasks we haven't done and the uncertainty of not having an overview of what we want to achieve.

Terrific time managers are generally physically fit people who exercise regularly. Scientists Daniel Landers of Arizona State

University and George Chrousos of the US National Institute of Health surveyed research into the effects of exercise and found that people are in a better mood and think faster during and after exercise than at other times. Exercise increases levels of hormones called 'endorphins', which produce a sensation of euphoria, and 'cortisone', which wakes us up. These changes could lead to a sense of well-being that bolsters productivity.

Exercise is the 'feel better' phenomenon.

- Exercise for *stamina*, *strength*, and *suppleness*.
- Exercise to increase your *self-confidence* and *self-esteem*.
- Exercise to improve your *mood*.
  Cosmonauts in the Russian space program initially reported depression when inactive during space flights. When they were put on a regular exercise program, their depression evaporated.
- Exercise to reduce your *stress* levels.
  Dr Herbert de Vries compared the effects of exercise with tranquillisers and found that even as little exercise as a 15-minute walk is more relaxing than a tranquilliser!

How much exercise? This varies from person to person, but Chrousos recommends a relatively vigorous activity like running or swimming three times a week. Experiment to find the level of exercise that makes you feel both physically and psychologically 'well'.

Be goal-guided, not goal-governed

Do you routinely establish goals for yourself?

Psychologists Richard Guzzo of New York University, Ellen Langer of Harvard, and Edwin Locke of the University of Maryland have found that goal setting increases productivity in terms of both quality and quantity more than any other technique, including pay increases! If you want to accomplish anything, set explicit and challenging goals. Aiming for easy or vague goals will do little for your productivity. Make them important and worthwhile, too, so that you will be committed to them.

If you haven't developed a personal vision, go back to Chapter 2 and *do it now!* Mould your aspirations and intentions into specific goals and action plans. Commit to your aims. Since short-term goals make long-term goals seem more real and achievable and are easier to work to, break up large and longer-term goals into weekly and daily goals. Daily or weekly plans or To Do lists are ideal for this.

Paul Meyer, President of Success Motivation International says:

> *'Success is the progressive realisation of worthwhile,*
> *pre-determined goals.'*

Use your goals to guide your actions, not rule them. Blind pursuit of any one goal can be counter-productive since the initial course you set to reach a goal may not turn out to be the most fruitful. We need to keep an open mind.

Being goal-guided helps us do this. A goal-governed journalist, for example, might conduct an interview based on prepared questions, even if the interviewee began to reveal something off-track but more interesting. A goal-guided journalist would listen, think and explore instead of blindly following and scribbling.

Would you call yourself a flexible, creative thinker or is your mind more like a railroad train going straight down the tracks towards its goal?

If you're a terrific time manager, you're likely to be a goal-governed, creative, flexible thinker who can turn stumbling blocks into building blocks, find innovative solutions to the same old problems and continually find new and better ways to work towards your goals.

Railroad track thinkers do things automatically and mindlessly, which causes them to miss opportunities. This kind of thinking also leads to burnout.

Have some fun!

During a typical working day do you take a break every once in a while to relax or do something you enjoy, or do you slog hard at it until knocking off time?

Poor time managers are often obsessed with busy-ness. If you're a terrific time manager, you probably find ways to bring fun into your work and take regular breaks. This helps revitalise your brain, energy level and thinking processes. Psychologist Stephen Colarelli of Central Michigan University and health educator Allan Luks say that rest and reflection are crucial to productivity.

Some of the most productive public figures took time to rest. Winston Churchill, for example, took one long nap almost every day, even during World War II. Albert Einstein 'discovered' the theory of relativity while daydreaming in a meadow.

Rest is good. So is laughter. Laughter helps us relax and improves our creativity while humour helps us lose ourselves in what we're doing.

William Fry Jr, MD, the 'Doctor of Humour' who has researched the power of humour for over 30 years, believes that laughter is a total body experience, an 'internal massage'. It involves all the body's systems including muscles, nerves, brain and digestion. After being stimulated and exercised by laughter, the body goes into deep relaxation. Like jogging, laughter is a good aerobic exercise. It aerates the lungs, relaxes the muscles, nerves and heart, expands breathing and circulation, and enhances oxygen intake and expenditure. He says:

'100 to 200 laughs equals 10 minutes rowing and jogging.'

Are you using enough humour to help keep yourself on track?

If laughter heals, think what 'lightening up' a bit will do for your time management!

THE POWER OF LAUGHTER

In 1964, Norman Cousins was given a one in 500 chance of recovering from a rare spinal disease called 'ankylosing spondylitis'. Within days, he could barely move his arms and legs and his jaws nearly seized. He found that ten minutes of genuine belly laughing gave him two hours pain-free sleep.

Subsequent research has confirmed the release role of endorphins and enkephalins (two natural pain suppressers) through laughter.

Look at your environment

Do you 'call the shots'?

Psychologist Stephen Colarelli of Central Michigan University has found that internal factors aren't the only influences on how much a person can get done. It's also important to consider the environment, especially the degree of decision-making freedom people have; this has much more to do with performance than IQ or background.

If you're burdened by too much boss-imposed and system-imposed time (see Chapter 6), if monkeys are managing your time (see Chapter 4), or if you feel pulled in all directions, find some ways to claim more discretionary time. This will not only improve your ability to manage your time to achieve things that are important to you, but will also increase your self-confidence and self-esteem.

Do you really know whether you're doing your job well? How do you know your life is fulfilling your expectations, wants and needs?

Another crucial element to achieving our goals is feedback. You need to know how you're doing. At work, ask yourself:

- Does my manager provide me with increasing levels of responsibility?
- Are my customers satisfied?
- Am I achieving in my Key Result Areas?

In your personal life, ask yourself:

- Am I living my life in line with my most important values?
- Am I achieving my personal vision and goals in each of my key life roles and life facets?
- Do I make enough time for myself and for the key people in my life?

Even if your environment is less than inspiring, there are plenty of things you can do to be more productive personally: a healthy lifestyle, an optimistic, flexible outlook, and effective time management will all help you to accomplish more.

Do you establish a culture of excellence? If you do, it will inspire peak performance and productivity. Focus on the challenge of each task and draw on the enthusiasm and drive generated by the best of those around you. Productivity and time management is, in short, largely a personal matter.

> 'Keep away from people who try to belittle your ambitions. Small people always do that but the really great make you feel that you, too, can become great.'
>
> *Mark Twain, 1835–1910*
> *US author and humorist*

Stay in control

Do you focus on things within your control or beyond your control?

You can't control events, but you can control your reactions to them. Your budget, the competition and the economy are important, but you have no power over them. Focus on what you can control and influence and don't let the things outside of your control get under your skin.

If something goes wrong, do you pretend it hasn't happened, look for someone or something to blame, or search for excuses? Or do you take responsibility and look for ways to fix the problem?

If you're a terrific time manager, you will look towards the future, not the past, and find ways to fix problems. You know that apportioning blame or making excuses merely wastes time.

Take responsibility for making your time count. Don't wait for others or outside events to do it for you. Don't blame others or outside events, either. Making time is in your hands: no excuses!

Do you have high self-esteem?

High self-esteem helps us stay in control and take responsibility for making things happen. It helps us prevent outside events and 'emergencies' from controlling our moods and how we use our time. It helps us to be Proactive, call the shots, and spend our time in Quadrant 1 (see Chapter 4).

Watch your thoughts; they become words.
Watch your words; they become actions.
Watch your actions; they become habits.
Watch your habits; they become character.
Watch your character; it becomes your destiny.
Frank Outlaw

CHAPTER **19**

Make your mind work for you

How to harness the power of your subconscious to make time

SHH... HE'S WORKING

Z

Research into peak performance shows that at least 50 per cent of an athlete's performance success, and an even higher percentage of performance failures and errors, are due to mental factors. We're not talking about how smart they are, but about things like their attitudes and mindsets, the way they talk to themselves, and the way they see themselves doing things. In short, we're talking about the way they employ the vast power of their subconscious.

What holds true for sports people and athletes holds true in other walks of life, including time management.

In this chapter, you will discover how to help your subconscious work energetically and forcefully on your behalf as you work towards making time. You will learn how to 'program' your subconscious to support your efforts, how to harness its power to literally re-program and strengthen your brain and guide your behaviour, and how to maximise its potential so that you effortlessly automatically manage your time well and achieve your goals.

Our conscious and subconscious minds

Our conscious mind works only when we're awake. It uses logic and creativity to make decisions, analyse information, set goals, make plans, think things through. It can deal with up to ten things at once, provided they are routine and familiar (for example, driving a car or making a cup of coffee), although concentrating fully on more than one thing at a time overloads it.

Our subconscious can deal with an infinite number of things at the same time. It works constantly, even when we're asleep. It retains everything that happens to us, everything we see, experience and feel, to provide an endless pool of information, insights and conclusions. Consciously or unconsciously, through reasoning things out or through a sudden burst of intuition or insight, we draw on this vast storehouse to guide our behaviour and achieve our objectives.

This makes our subconscious mind by far the more powerful,

subtle and influential of the two. It is programmed to help us out. Perhaps that's why it continually tries to transmit information and ideas to our conscious mind.

The subconscious informs

How well do you receive messages from your subconscious? Some people receive them better than others. The more preoccupied, stressed, harassed and confused your conscious mind is, the less well it can receive information from your subconscious. That's one compelling reason we need Make Time techniques to bring order to our lives (through job purpose, Key Result Areas, clear goals, To Do lists, and so on).

DREAM YOUR WAY TO SUCCESS

Do you think dreaming is for kids? Think again.

Consider these Nobel Prize winners and what dreaming did for them:

Neils Bohr, the Danish physicist who discovered that the atomic structure resembles the solar system and developed the Bohr atomic model of an atomic nucleus surrounded by orbiting electrons, first saw his model in a dream.

Otto Lowei won his prize in physiology for proving that nerve impulses are transmitted both electrically and chemically through an experiment on frogs. He dreamed this experiment on three successive nights before actually conducting it.

Fredrick Kekule developed his theory of closed atomic chains from a daydream he had on a London bus. In another dream, he figured out the ring structure of the Benzene molecule.

Consider these artists:

Robert Louis Stevenson received a mountain of rejections on his manuscript on the duel nature of man. He then dreamed three scenes central to the plot of *Dr Jeckyll and Mr Hyde* and rewrote his now-classic novel.

> *Jean Depré*, the French painter of *Pieta* fell asleep while thinking about where to position Christ. He saw the placement of Christ and his disciples in a dream and painted his famous painting.
>
> Consider these business people:
>
> *Carl Duisberg*, of German paint manufacturer IG-Farben Co, fell asleep in his office and dreamed a process to produce a blue pigment of superior quality. It worked and both he and his company reaped huge financial rewards.
>
> *Conrad Hilton* wanted to buy a company that was for sale by silent auction. He dreamed the sale price and submitted it the night before bids closed. He won the bid, beating his next nearest bidder by only $2,000. He sold the company a few years later for a $2 million profit.

How can you receive information from your subconscious in a dream? The process is called 'incubation'. As you are falling asleep, think about, for example, a problem you are working on. What do you know about it already? What do you need to know? What do you want its solution to offer? Then go to sleep and let your subconscious work on it.

Eight out of ten times, you will get an answer within three nights of incubation. It will pop into your mind upon wakening or during the day.

The subconscious communicates with us in other ways too. Have you ever had a flash of insight or intuition? Has something you were trying to remember ever suddenly 'popped' into your mind? Have you ever done or said something without knowing why and it turned out to be just the right thing to do or say? That was your subconscious talking to you. From its vast information storehouse, it can forewarn us, caution us, alert us, guide us, and teach us.

Making it easier for our subconscious mind to work for us, in any sphere of life, not just making time, will increase our effectiveness and success. *Actively* helping it to do so will vastly increase our effectiveness and success.

The subconscious orchestrates

The subconscious is also important for another reason: it is used to having its own way. If something our conscious mind is trying to do conflicts with values, beliefs or attitudes buried in our subconscious, our subconscious will find ways to sabotage our conscious efforts and fulfil our subconscious desires and beliefs.

> *The subconscious isn't just a storehouse.*
> *It's also an implementer.*

How could our subconscious work against our conscious intentions? This can happen in three ways.

Values clash

If our conscious intentions aren't aligned with our values—that is, if they jar with each other—the values will take precedence. Our subconscious will find ways to make us behave in line with our values, not our stated intentions. Our resulting behaviour may puzzle others and ourselves and may be a source of concern, irritation, or even conflict.

CLASHING VALUES

Meng wanted to get her own work done but never seemed to find enough hours in the day. Then she found that one of her core values was helping others. This explained why she found it difficult to rid herself of monkeys.

Once she realised she could best serve others by helping them to work things out for themselves and take responsibility for completing their own tasks, she was able to get on top of her job.

Paul had trouble getting everything done, too. He found his core values revolved around having fun, friendship and being part of a group. It's no wonder he had trouble dealing with visitors, telephone interruptions, and sticking to the agenda in meetings.

197

This was made worse by the fact that he worked in an open plan office, which, to him, literally cried out 'Party!'

Once he realised what was happening, he was able to make a concerted effort to focus his attention on his job and Value-adding activities. He satisfied his high-priority needs for 'socialising' by having lunch more often with colleagues, chatting with them while he attended to routine matters, and getting together with friends after hours. (His workmates appreciated his new approach, too.)

Gwen found two of her core values were reliability and discipline. This made it easy for her to keep her commitments, focus on Value-adding tasks, and say 'No' when necessary in order to get through her To Do list. Unfortunately, it also helped explain why others sometimes saw her as rigid and remote.

She decided to work on being more approachable. Even when she was busy, she decided to make time to chat to her co-workers.

Theo had a core value of perfection. This meant he often did things better than the task itself warranted. He always ran out of time and as a result worked excessive overtime. Value-adding tasks sat undone while Marginal tasks were completed to perfection.

Theo needed to learn to prioritise and know when close enough was good enough and when it wasn't. Once he did, he found he was accomplishing everything he needed to at work in far less time. This gave him more time to spend working on his personal goals.

(If you need to find out more about your own core values, see pages 8–11 in Chapter 2.)

Beliefs clash

If our deep-seated beliefs about others or ourselves are at odds with our statements, the former will prevail. Our subconscious will conspire to make sure our actions support our deeper beliefs. This is why people may 'say' one thing and 'do' another.

CLASHING BELIEFS

Jade's self-image was one of ineptitude. Whatever she was confronted with, her thoughts went automatically to 'I can't', not 'I can'. Her low self-confidence meant her expectations about what she could achieve were low. Although she *wanted* to be capable, her deeper beliefs were stronger. Her subconscious made sure she fulfilled her own (worst) expectations. She never managed to get through the Value-adding items on her To Do list and when challenged with difficult tasks she felt overwhelmed and powerless to get through them.

Geoff had low self-esteem, too. Therefore he always took on the easy jobs and left the hard ones (believing he couldn't do them). As a result, he never learned new things, developed his skills, or pushed his personal envelope. If he tried to, his subconscious made sure the results were in keeping with his deep-seated beliefs about himself. He would fail. Why bother becoming a better time manager?

Manju, on the other hand, had positive expectations of herself which showed as a 'can do' approach and a willingness to tackle anything. She didn't say 'I can't do this' but 'I can't do this yet'. When she had a go at something new, she said: 'It may not be perfect first time 'round, but I'll give it my best shot.' People knew they could depend on Manju. She saw mistakes as learning opportunities and obstacles as stepping-stones. Her optimistic beliefs about herself provided the subconscious support she needed to get things done.

Chan saw most people as incompetent. He had trouble delegating tasks because, after all, 'No-one can do it as well as I can'. If one of his team had a problem, he took over and did it for them. This made him a 'soft touch' and resulted in monkeys crawling all over him. Poor Chan's frenzied work pace was him getting nowhere and beginning to take a toll on his health. His subconscious belief 'They can't!' continually undermined his best efforts to try and let people help him out and do things for themselves.

Mindsets clash

In Chapter 18 we discussed the mindsets of terrific time managers. If our mindsets don't support making time, they are probably working against it.

CLASHING MINDSETS

David had a mindset of 'sticking to the plan'. This meant he was goal-governed. A great believer in 'the power of the plan', he had trouble deviating from his selected course of action even when it became apparent that it wasn't working. This career-limiting mindset resulted in mistakes, wasted time and effort, and frustration for David and everyone around him.

Our subconscious has immense power to help us or to hinder us. Here are three ways to harness its power and make it work for you. Each one works. Used in combination, they are awesome!

Self-talk

If you talk to yourself, are you crazy? Hardly. Psychologists estimate that we talk to ourselves 60,000 times a day. That's pretty non-stop. (To save you the calculation, there are only 86,400 seconds in a day.)

These silent messages can be full-blown conversations ('Shall I do this now, or later? Oh, I'd rather do it later. Although really I should do it now and get it over with. But . . . ') or they may be instantaneous, lasting only a fraction of a second. Either way, they permeate our subconscious, which proceeds to execute them.

'The greatest discovery of my generation is that human beings can alter their lives by altering their state of mind.'

William James said this over 100 years ago. Often called the founder of modern psychology, he thought he was speaking only about our thoughts. He didn't realise what he said was also true physically.

Although part of our subconscious, we now know that our mindsets and self-talk have a physical aspect, too.

OUR AMAZING BRAIN

We have an estimated ten billion nerves in our brain. With chemicals and electricity, each can make thousands of possible links to our 100 billion neurones, or brain cells. The number of connections inside our brain is greater than the known number of atoms in the entire universe. Every time we think a thought, it links a unique pathway of neurons.

Self-talk strengthens pathways, or neural circuits—millions of brain cells firing together—in our brain. This means that the more often we think something, the more ingrained that thought becomes and the more likely we are to think it again.

Our subconscious doesn't assess whether our self-talk is right or wrong, good or bad, helpful or not. It simply acts on it. If you continually tell yourself 'I'm disorganised!' your subconscious will, in effect, respond: 'Oh, okay, I'll find you lots of disorganised ways to behave.'

Self-talk guides our behaviour and shapes our success.

Instead of saying . . .	Say . . .
I'll never get through all this!	I'll tackle things one at a time, starting with the most important.
I'm such a messy person!	I'll take the time to tidy things up now.
This is too big a job to tackle now.	I'll break this into small bite-sized chunks and make a start.
I don't know where to begin.	I'll assess what needs to be done and do what adds the most value first.

What silent messages about time management do you give yourself? As my friend Steven Koski says:

'The loudest voice you'll ever hear is your own.'

HARNESS THE POWER
OF YOUR SELF-TALK

Do you want to improve your time management? Listen to your self-talk and make sure it supports your conscious intentions. If it doesn't, silence it and replace it with a positive, helpful message. Paint the picture you want to achieve. Imbed it in your subconscious and it will become reality.

Change your self-talk, change your behaviour.

Make sure you replace unhelpful self-talk with a positive message. In other words,

Say what you do *want, not what you* don't *want.*

Why? Our subconscious ignores negatives. If you say 'I never panic when I have a lot to do', your subconscious will act on 'I panic when I have a lot to do'! Quite a difference!

Mind your language when you talk to yourself!

Insist that your self-talk supports your efforts at making time, not sabotages them.

Affirmations

Do you know that you can consciously program your subconscious to support your efforts to make time? You can do this with affirmations.

Affirmations are a special type of self-talk. Although self-talk is generally spontaneous, affirmations are deliberate. With affirmations, we can consciously direct our thoughts to re-program our attitudes, beliefs and behaviour. Here's how it works.

Affirmations literally build and then strengthen neural pathways in our brain. The more we affirm something, the more these circuits ignite and the stronger they become. Eventually, they fire automatically and we find ourselves acting on them. How long does this take? Most people report noticeable results in about three weeks.

Affirmations are strong, first person, present tense statements that describe the behaviour you want to build. Use positive language and, if possible, include not just the behaviour but how you feel when you behave in the way described.

Make your affirmations easy to remember so you can carry them around 'in your head' with you and repeat them every chance you get, at least twice a day. The most effective times are just as you wake up and just as you are going to sleep, when your brain is relaxed and in a more receptive state.

It's best to write your own affirmations because you know just what you need to re-program. Here are some examples to help you get started:

- Do you want to become better organised? Here's an affirmation that may help:
  I enjoy taking the time to sort things out and put things away.
- Does chaos follow you around? Try this affirmation:
  I effortlessly turn chaos into order.
- Do you have a tendency to procrastinate? Try affirming this:
  Do it now! is my motto.

- Do you find that you waste a lot of time waiting for others? Perhaps an affirmation along these lines will help:

  I easily find something useful to do while I wait.

- Do you do things as they crop up instead of setting priorities? This affirmation might work:

  I relish thinking things through and making workable
  plans based on my priorities.

- Perhaps a ringing telephone sends you rushing to answer it, much as Pavlov's dogs salivated at the sound of a bell. If so, try this:

  I treat the telephone as a tool for my convenience,
  not the other way around.

Take care not to overload your subconscious with affirmations. Six at a time is probably enough. Try writing them on index cards and flicking through them until you get to know them.

Strengthen your affirmations by seeing and feeling them in your mind's eye as you repeat them. The more you do this, the more powerfully you program your subconscious, which then finds ways to make your affirmations come true.

Use affirmations to harness the power of your subconscious to build your self-image as someone who manages their time with grace and ease.

Visualising

Make a plan

Don't just say: 'From now on, I'm going to use practical time management techniques to make time.' What specifically are you going to do?

Follow the tips in Chapter 17 for building *Make Time* habits. Choose from the array of tips in Part 3 of this book and write down the ones you intend to try out first, and when. Writing them down will fix them in your subconscious and exponentially increase the likelihood that you will apply them successfully.

Do it now! Then work confidently and consistently towards implementing them.

Now that you have planned specifically which *Make Time* tips you are going to try out, it's time to visualise yourself applying them successfully.

Visualise it

What mental images do you have about yourself, and more specifically, about the way you manage your time? Visualisation is about making mental imagery work for you. It's about using your mind's eye to program your subconscious to direct your behaviour to achieve the outcomes you want.

Visualisation programs your body to do exactly what you see in your mind's eye. It works because if you do something once, even in your mind, you've built a mental pathway. This makes it easier to do it a second time. This is how you can turn an average performance into an unbelievable performance!

Do you want to be able to say 'No' nicely when you already have a million things to do and someone asks for your time? Do you want to improve your personal organisation, sort out chaos, or stop procrastinating? Do you want to manage meetings masterfully, delegate proficiently, or discourage drop-in visitors? Visualising can help you do it. You'll be able to do all these things and more, if you mentally rehearse doing *exactly* what you want to do, perfectly.

PURE PERFECTION

Have you noticed any Olympians staring into space with a fixed gaze just before their 'performance'? They were visualising. And they certainly didn't wait until just before the event to visualise their perfect performance. They were almost certainly visualising every last detail of the event and how they intended to compete in it, on their way to the venue and at least once a day for most of the period of their training. By the time they actually competed, they'd already 'run their race' a million times.

205

Top athletes, team and individual sports people, all rehearse perfect performance. In fact, visualisation and the other mental techniques we look at in this chapter are now essential elements in an elite athlete's sports kit.

Just as visualisation can affect an elite athlete's performance, it can affect behaviour in other fields of life. It will even help us make time.

How can just imagining something possibly make it come true? Like affirmations, visualisation affects the brain and, therefore, the body. Visualisation makes the connections between the cells in our brain fire, just as they do when we physically perform an activity. It builds and strengthens our brain circuits so much that the behaviour we visualise becomes automatic. This is what neurologist Ian Robertson, of Trinity College, Dublin, calls 'sculpting the brain'.

Most neuroscientists, or brain scientists, agree. Visualisation activates neural circuits in the same way that physical performance activates them. And they activate the *same* circuits. This means that the brain doesn't know the difference between mental performance and physical performance. (In fact, if you are visualising yourself doing something particularly strenuous, you will end up feeling physically exhausted!)

Visualise yourself employing *Make Time* habits to activate your brain and build a supporting neural network. This makes it easier to apply these habits in real life.

'Mental practice can
actually increase real-world
strength and performance.'

Ian Robertson, neurologist
Author of Mind Sculpture

THE MIND–BODY LINK

Stephen Kosslyn of Harvard University, researching how visualisation actually works, asked people to imagine tensing and relaxing the muscles of their right index finger, but without actually moving it. They did this for several minutes every day. Four weeks later, the strength of their finger had increased by 20 per cent. Making the neural connections mentally was just as effective as making them physically. Visualisation causes physical changes in the brain in the same way that physical effort does, whether it's strengthening muscles, swinging a golf club well, or managing your time better.

According to Karl Pibram, a neurophysiologist at Stanford University, mental rehearsal stimulates the neurology and results in micro muscle movements. It helps us to have great and positive expectations. And, by imbedding in our minds what we see, hear, and feel in our mental practice, it gives us a clear target to aim at.

HOW TO VISUALISE

When you visualise, do so intensely and with focused concentration. Unless you do this, the effects will be marginal. To really strengthen those neural circuits and engage your powerful subconscious, make your mental practice powerful and vigorous.

The more intensely you visualise, the more rapidly you can make particular sets of synapses fire. The more often you make them fire, the stronger they become and the more likely they are to propel you into your Flow Zone (see below, 'Get in the Zone!').

The better you're able to sculpt your brain through visualising, the more your subconscious will take over and execute your visualised performance for you. You will have less to think about consciously. You'll coast through on automatic pilot and free up your conscious mind for other things.

Since we strengthen our mental circuits whenever we do something perfectly in our mind's eye, visualise often.

You'll be able to do a million things at once and not go crazy!

How can you use visualisation to manage your time better? Select a Make Time technique from Part 3. As often as you can, at least once a day, see yourself doing it. Strengthen it by repeating a supporting affirmation before and after you visualise. When you do it 'for real', repeat your affirmation, if appropriate. Keep affirming and visualising and doing it 'for real' until the habit is built and the new behaviour becomes second nature.

SAYING 'NO' NICELY

Jan wanted to be able to say 'No' nicely and feel good about it. At the same time, she also wanted to maintain a cooperative relationship with the person concerned. She thought of several typical situations when people ask her to do something and she feels pressured to say 'Yes' when really she would like to say 'No' and get on with her own work.

She chose three of these to work on. First, she decided what she would say in each one. Then she mentally rehearsed all the details: where she would be, who she would be speaking with, what they would be asking and how they would be asking it, what she would say and how she would say it, how she would feel as she said it (confident and in charge), and her body language. She made sure her feelings were positive.

After several intensive sessions of visualising herself in these situations, doing, saying and feeling what she wanted to do, say and feel with perfection, she felt confident enough to 'have a go' in real life. She found that steadily (and not without some effort) she was, indeed, able to say 'No' confidently, maintain cooperative relationships, and get her own work done. What a relief! As this gradually became automatic, Jan also found she had earned a bit more respect from others!

When you visualise, you can take a 'bird's eye view' and watch yourself. For example, you can make a mental movie and watch yourself on a cinema or TV screen. Another way is to actually step inside yourself and see yourself doing it from the inside out. Try them both and see which you find easier and which works best for you.

Six simple steps to success

Here are six steps to follow to visualise your way to success:

Verbalise it

1 *Set a clear and worthwhile goal.* Write it down to fix it in your subconscious.

Visualise it

2 *Relax.* Focus on taking two or three deep breaths and relaxing your muscles.

3 *Concentrate on your goal.* See yourself doing whatever it is that you need to do to attain it. Picture as much detail as possible—who will be there, where you will be, what you will be seeing—as you do whatever it is you're visualising yourself doing.

Sensualise it

4 *Engage your senses.* What will you be hearing, smelling, saying as you do whatever it is you're visualising yourself doing?

Emotionalise it

5 *Engage your emotions.* How are you feeling as you're working towards your goal? How are you feeling when you reach your goal? Capture those feelings and savour them.

Revise it

6 *Visualise this over and over*, as often as possible. Do this at least once a day. Twice would be better.

PAUL MENDS HIS WAYS
(AND SAVES HIS JOB)

Paul's disorganisation was legendary. He was a familiar sight scurrying around the office, shirt tail hanging out, in a flat spin. Late for a meeting, late with a report, compiling equipment in a last-minute panic: 'Can't stop to chat—must rush!' Why was it, if he was always so busy, that he never managed to achieve anything?

His boss told him he needed to put some simple systems in place so he would know what to do when, and where to find things.

So he bought a book on how to make time. He found out how to prioritise according to his job purpose and Key Result Areas and how to make time for his personal goals. Because he was not a 'morning person', he visualised feeling 'on top of things' as he organised and prioritised his To Do list every evening before he left work. Paul also visualised himself arriving at work and confidently getting started straight away on Value-adding activities. After a while, with repeated visualisations and affirmations supporting 'the real thing', operating according to his To Do list became second nature. The more he achieved, the better he felt. Slowly, others began to see Paul as a person who actually *did* get things done!

Paul also discovered he needed to organise his desk and filing system. Since his was a particularly serious case, he asked a secretary to help him out. With her coaching and occasional prodding, he became used to putting things away, filing documents correctly, and *loving* the results!

The third and final change Paul made, in his first of many rounds of improving his time management, was to make an effort to get to meetings on time. He visualised himself gathering his papers, getting up and leaving his desk when it was time to go to a meeting, and feeling professional and reliable when he arrived on time.

He also began to change the way he used his electronic diary. When he noted a meeting in it, along with the time and place, he also worked backwards and noted down when he would need to leave for the meeting and when he would need to begin preparing for it. Last-minute panics vanished. When his diary beeped to tell him it was time to prepare for a meeting, he prepared for it. When it beeped to tell him it was time to leave for a meeting, he got up and left! Others were at first surprised, but slowly came to change their view of Paul to someone who could be relied on.

MIND OVER MATTER

'Weight-lifting is all 'mind over matter'. As long as the mind can envision the fact that you can do something, you can . . .
I visualised myself being there already—having achieved the goal already. Working out is just the physical follow-through, a reminder of the vision you're focusing on.'

Arnold Schwarzenegger
Cited in *Superlearning*, Dell Publishing

'Those neurones that fire together wire together. Every thought we have makes new connections as well as reconstructs old ones. We can change our brain function, and the patterns of our behaviour, ourselves.'

Evian Gordon, brain scientist,
Westmead Hospital, Sydney

It has been said that our brains work in a similar way to computers. The GIGO principle certainly seems to hold true for both:

Garbage In—Garbage Out.

Make sure to program your brain with gold, not garbage!

Get in The Zone!

Have you ever done something extraordinarily well and got exceptional results? Did your body seem to take over and you operated on automatic pilot? Perhaps you were even aware that if you stopped to think about what you were doing, you'd 'blow it'. If so, you were in what's referred to as the Flow Zone, or simply, The Zone. This is the mental state that produces peak performance.

The Zone is well known in sports all over the world. When sports people get in The Zone they achieve their personal best and win medals. According to psychologist Mihaly Czikszentmihalyi, the Flow Zone is characterised by intense yet relaxed, calm concentration. Tension and anxiety are low, oxygen intake is reduced, breathing is regular, muscles are loose and our brain waves enter the relaxed alpha rhythm when we're in The Zone. We easily concentrate on our specific goal and resist distractions.

When we're in The Zone, our subconscious takes over and produces the performance we have visualised over and over again. Our brain switches to automatic pilot and those peak-performing circuits fire unconsciously, making success easy and effortless.

In fact, working from The Zone practically guarantees us a successful outcome. The more often we get in The Zone, the more often we will achieve the results we're after. We can apply Flow Zone techniques to make time, too. Visualisation can help us attain it, and technology and better time management can help us keep it.

In time management terms, interruptions can be deadly. Imagine being in your Flow Zone as you're developing an idea and the phone rings or someone knocks at your door! Ideas evaporate.

Modern technology can help us. We can switch on our answering machine and turn the telephone ringer to silent, we can take our work somewhere we won't be disturbed, and we can put on headphones as we work to discourage interruptions and 'visitors'.

In most cases, though, we probably need to help ourselves. If you want to work from your Flow Zone and find that your surroundings hold you back, learn to tune them out.

Stay out of the Drone Zone

When we're caught up in meaningless, mundane, Marginal tasks that don't contribute any value to our lives, we're in the Drone Zone. We end up feeling tired and bored and performing poorly. We behave mindlessly, not mindfully.

Stay out of the Drone Zone by continuously focusing on your goals and priorities, in both your personal and working life. Work on Value-adding activities as much as you can and feel good about what you are accomplishing. Stay away from as many Marginal activities as you can and when you must do them, do them because you *want* to, not because you have to. In short, get in the habit of applying the mindsets of terrific time managers described in Chapter 18.

Stay out of the Panic Zone

When we're feeling anxious and unsure about what we're doing, and constantly wondering what to do next, we may be in the Panic Zone. Our brain releases hormones that cause our muscles to tense. Our heart beats more rapidly and our body temperature rises. We need to put in a lot of effort before we see any results.

If you want to stay out of the Panic Zone, make sure you don't get caught up in any of the time management myths and apply the Make Time principles described in Chapter 7. And while it's important to focus on your goals, don't focus exclusively on the future. Set clear, challenging and achievable goals, keep them in sight, and enjoy yourself as you make progress towards them.

Perhaps you're worrying about something that might happen and this is stopping you from getting on with things. Remember that whatever we focus on expands. If we keep worrying about something, we'll actively create a self-fulfilling prophecy, making sure that it will happen.

How do you put it out of your mind? Focus on your goal, on what you want to happen, not the obstacles. There will always be obstacles. What makes the difference is how we view them. Finally, apply the techniques discussed in this chapter to engage the vast power of your subconscious to help you.

Maximise the potential of your subconscious brain

Follow these six great tips to really ramp up the power of your subconscious.

Have a vision—set goals. We discussed the importance of goal setting and how to set clear and compelling goals in Chapter 2. If you haven't done so already, now would be a good time to review this chapter and write down some realistic yet challenging goals. This will imbed them in your subconscious and help you achieve them.

Learn to see problems and goals clearly. Review and apply the information in Chapters 2 and 18.

Write down your ideas the moment they occur to you. This takes a load off your conscious brain and opens the channels of communication with your subconscious.

'What concerns me
most about stress is not that
it kills, but that it prevents
one from savouring life.'

Hans Serle, stress researcher

Set aside time for relaxing. As we saw earlier, it's difficult to communicate with our subconscious when we're stressed and harried.

Improved time management often results in a reduction in stress levels, which in turns helps our subconscious to help us. Use whatever stress reduction techniques work for you. Good long-term techniques include exercise, meditation, yoga, and autogenic training. Alcohol and drugs are poor short-term techniques.

Create variety in your life. This keeps your neural pathways flexible and open.

Create structure and overview. Many of the Make Time tips and principles are targeted at helping you create structure and overview. This helps you focus on what you need to do to achieve results, get into your Flow Zone and stay out of your Panic and Drone Zones.

Boost the effectiveness of your efforts to *Make Time* by helping your subconscious mind work for you.

215

A final word

CHAPTER 20

How to continue making time long after you close this book

You know how to focus your efforts and energy on high priority, big pay-off tasks. You also know how to get more Value-adding things done in less time. This will free up some of your time to do the things you want to do; some of the personal goals you set for yourself in Chapter 2.

Terrific, isn't it?

Don't follow the tips mindlessly, though! Adapt the techniques suggested in this book and apply them in your own way. Focus on the Make Time principles and mindsets and find ways to do what works best for you.

Keep adding to your arsenal of Make Time techniques by dipping back into this book frequently. Even if you only do this in a few minutes of down time, you may find another idea you want to try out.

'Time is infinitely more precious than money and there is nothing common between them. You cannot accumulate time; you cannot borrow time; you can never tell how much time you have left in the Bank of Life. Time is life.'

Israel Davidson, writer

Keep it up

To keep up the good work, do these three things:

1 Stay focused on your goals and Key Result Areas.

2 Don't let yourself backslide into poor time management habits.

3 Once a year, review and update your personal vision for a balanced life. What have you accomplished? What has helped you? What has held you back?

Update your vision for the next 12 months, setting annual, six-monthly and monthly goals in each facet of your life. Keep your goals handy, refer to them often, and *go for it*!

Commit

You know the techniques. You know how to find your purpose, so you can work on the right things, and you know how to practise Make Time techniques to do things efficiently.

Perhaps you've already started. Fantastic! If you haven't, what's stopping you? How about starting now?

One of the main differences between people who succeed and people who don't is commitment. If you're *really* committed to making time, you will have already begun. If you haven't begun yet, start acting on what you have read in this book as soon as you put it down.

If you only wanted to learn about how to manage your time better, well, you've done that! The question is, what will

> 'If you want a quality, act as if you already had it.'
>
> *William James, 1842–1910*
> *US psychologist*

you do with your knowledge? How will you put it to use? *Will* you put it to use?

We all die; it's how we live our life that counts. To live a life we enjoy and are proud of, we need to manage our time carefully and well.

Good luck!

Is what you're doing right now the best use of your time?

'Time is the best teacher. Unfortunately, it kills all of its students.'

Author unknown

You have only just a minute,
Only sixty seconds in it.
Forced upon you, can't refuse it;
Didn't seek it; didn't choose it.
But it's up to you to use it.
You must suffer if you lose it;
Give account if you abuse it.
Just a tiny little minute
But an eternity is in it.

Author unknown

Bibliography

Books

Carlson, Richard, *Don't Sweat the Small Stuff*, Hyperion, 1997

Cole, Kris, *Supervision: The Theory and Practice of First Line Management*, Prentice Hall, second edition, 2001

Cole, Kris, *Crystal Clear Communication*, Prentice Hall, second edition, 2000

Drucker, Peter, *The Effective Executive*, Harperbusiness, 1993

Krass, Peter (ed), *The Book of Management Wisdom: Classic Writings by Legendary Managers*, John Wiley & Sons, 2000

Walters, D (ed), *Creative Innovators*, Royal Publishing, 1988

Journals and periodicals

Harvard Management Update, Harvard Business School Publishing newsletter

Harvard Business Review, Boston, Massachusetts